549.68 KEN
Kenner, Corrine, 1964-
Crystals for beginners
: a guide to collecting
& using stones &
AEPNL   30800005141186

D1013917

Crystals
for Beginners

NORTHERN LIGHTS LIBRARY SYSTEM
POSTAL BAG 8
ELK POINT, ALBERTA
T0A 1A0

photo ©Katherine Kenner

Corrine Kenner specializes in bringing metaphysical subjects down to earth. Her work on the tarot is widely published, and her classes and workshops are perennial favorites among students in the Midwest.

In addition to *Crystals for Beginners*, Corrine is the author of *Tall Dark Stranger*, a handbook on using tarot cards for romance; *Tarot Journaling*, a guide to the art of keeping a tarot diary; and *The Epicurean Tarot*. She also compiled an anthology of first-person stories called *Strange But True*. She is a certified tarot master, and she holds a bachelor's degree in philosophy from California State University, Long Beach.

Crystals
for *Beginners*

A Guide to Collecting & Using
Stones & Crystals

Corrine Kenner

Llewellyn Publications
Woodbury, Minnesota

Crystals for Beginners: A Guide to Collecting & Using Stones & Crystals © 2006 by Corrine Kenner. All rights reserved. No part of this book may be used or reproduced in any manner whatsoever, including Internet usage, without written permission from Llewellyn Publications except in the case of brief quotations embodied in critical articles and reviews.

First Edition
Second Printing, 2006

Book design and layout by Joanna Willis
Cover design by Gavin Dayton Duffy
Illustrations on pages 64–70, 72, 76–79, 159, 166 by Wendy Froshay
Illustrations on pages 118, 167 by Llewellyn art department

Llewellyn is a registered trademark of Llewellyn Worldwide, Ltd.

Library of Congress Cataloging-in-Publication Data
Kenner, Corrine, 1964–
    Crystals for beginners : a guide to collecting & using stones & crystals / Corrine Kenner.
        p. cm.
    Includes bibliographical references and index.
    ISBN-13: 978-0-7387-0755-6
    ISBN-10: 0-7387-0755-4
    1. Quartz—Collectors and collecting. 2. Quartz crystals—Psychic aspects. I. Title.

QE391.Q2K39 2006
549'.68—dc22

2006040963

Llewellyn Worldwide does not participate in, endorse, or have any authority or responsibility concerning private business transactions between our authors and the public.
    All mail addressed to the author is forwarded, but the publisher cannot, unless specifically instructed by the author, give out an address or phone number.
    Any Internet references contained in this work are current at publication time, but the publisher cannot guarantee that a specific location will continue to be maintained. Please refer to the publisher's website for links to authors' websites and other sources.

Llewellyn Publications
A Division of Llewellyn Worldwide, Ltd.
2143 Wooddale Drive, Dept. 0-7387-0755-4
Woodbury, MN 55125-2989, U.S.A.
www.llewellyn.com

Printed in the United States of America

Other Books in the For Beginners Series

Chakras for Beginners
David Pond

Divination for Beginners
Scott Cunningham

Healing Alternatives for Beginners
Kay Henrion

I Ching for Beginners
Mark McElroy

Meditation for Beginners
Stephanie Clement

Practical Magic for Beginners
Brandy Williams

Psychic Development for Beginners
William W. Hewitt

Contents

Introduction

People have always been fascinated by crystals. Since prehistoric hunters and gatherers first discovered quartz shining in a riverbed or flint glistening on a hillside, men and women have sought to incorporate crystals into their lives—both as objects of beauty, and as tools for the body, mind, and spirit.

Our early ancestors found innovative ways to craft stones and crystals into tools like knives, arrowheads, and fish hooks. While we no longer carve axes or chisels out of stone, we still depend on crystals as much as they ever did—and perhaps even more.

In fact, we rely on crystals more than any civilization in history. Like prehistoric people, we occasionally use crystals to start fires—we've simply updated the process, with relatively low-tech butane lighters. We also rely on crystals in building and manufacturing, and we have made them a main component of our communications equipment. Without crystals, our technology and our society would grind to a halt.

So, unlike our primitive ancestors, we don't simply pick up stones and crystals where we find them. Instead, we continually devise new techniques to discover new crystals, and we dig farther than ever to reach them. When we can't mine the crystals we need, we grow flawless specimens in a lab.

And just as early civilizations used crystals for divination, crystals still connect many of us to the divine.

Crystals certainly offer evidence of an intelligent creator—they are structured according to precise mathematical rules, and they adhere to clearly defined geometric patterns. For many, crystals offer tangible proof of God's perfection and God's plan.

Yet every crystal is unique, with properties and characteristics as varied as human beings. Crystals might even serve as a metaphor for human development. They are gestated deep within the earth, forced to grow under intense pressure, and made beautiful by extremes of time and temperature. And just like us, their interactions with the elements give them depth, and their flaws give them character.

In recent years, a number of spiritual practitioners have promoted the use of stones and crystals, particularly for healing. Crystals can be used for meditation, divination, and self-development.

This book will introduce you to the mystical world of crystals and give you the information you need to make crystals a part of your everyday life.

Lighter, Brighter, and Better

The Benefits of Working with Crystals

From agates to zoisite, the number of crystals on today's market can seem overwhelming. So can all of the powers attributed to all of those crystals.

Are you lonely? Grab yourself a rose quartz. Do your knees hurt? Try carrying some calcite along when you take a walk. Do you want to try your luck in Vegas? Don't forget your green aventurine.

No matter what ails you or what goal you have in sight, it seems that someone can recommend a crystal to cure all your ills or bring you good fortune. You could spend years reading and studying the encyclopedic books that have been written to describe the various metaphysical properties of crystals, stone by stone. And while it's true that individual crystals do have their own strengths, a surprising number of benefits can be attributed to *all* crystals. You don't have to memorize long lists of properties and associations to work with crystals—and you don't have to choose crystals based on anything in a book.

In fact, you will find that a long list of features and benefits can be assigned to every crystal—which makes choosing a stone for your own needs a lot less daunting.

The following properties apply to every crystal on earth:

- All crystals can help you balance your body, mind, and spirit.

- All crystals can receive and store energy. All crystals can also amplify that energy, focus it, and transmit it to others, at least to one degree or another.

- All crystals can make you feel safe and shielded from negative energy, and they can even help you feel more energetic yourself. There's nothing like plugging into a crystal for a few minutes to help you recharge your spiritual batteries.

- All crystals are grounding, because they originate deep within the womb of Mother Earth—which means that you can't get any closer to the ground than a crystal.

- All crystals, because they come from deep inside the earth, can help you tap into your own inner wisdom. Metaphorically speaking, all crystals can help you mine your buried reserves of energy and strength, and they can help you uncover your hidden talents.

- All crystals can help you calm and center your emotions so that you can pursue better health, better sleep, better thoughts, and better emotional well-being. Simply having crystals prominently displayed in your home or office can help create a more tranquil environment. At night, gazing into a crystal can help you relax, get to sleep faster, and enjoy a more restful night.

- All crystals can also help you develop a richer, more rewarding dream life, with happier dreams and better dream recall.

- All crystals can boost your confidence and self-esteem as amulets, talismans, or lucky charms.

- All crystals can be used as tools for insight and meditation; after all, there is a reason people have been gazing into crystal balls for centuries.

- All crystals can help you communicate with God and your higher self. A crystal's geometrically perfect structure and design are compelling evidence that God works with a plan. That connection to the divine can help you discover your destiny and feel more hopeful and optimistic about the future.

- All crystals can help you be more creative. When you combine your appreciation for beauty with an admiration of crystalline structure and symmetry, you will actually integrate the intuitive and rational sides of your mind—your logical left brain and your creative right brain.

- All crystals can help you develop your logical ability and analytical skills. Studying the mathematics of crystal formation will help you appreciate harmony, order, precision, and organization.

- All crystals can even inspire you to become more methodical, systematic, and self-disciplined. Your memory and willpower will improve, and you will have an easier time setting new goals for your life.

- All crystals can help you clarify your thoughts, and in the process, communicate them to other people. As you become better at expressing yourself, you will be better able to hold your ground in an argument and defend yourself from verbal attacks. You will become more assertive and more self-confident.

- All crystals can help you with your relationships. When you give crystals as gifts, they can help other people feel loved and appreciated. When you share your love of crystals with other people, the crystals can help you connect. Crystals are conversation pieces, if nothing else—but they can also help you coordinate your efforts, discover a rapport with others, and develop a sense of faithfulness and loyalty.

- All crystals can help you draw luck and good fortune into your life. Crystals can serve as beacons of energy and tangible reminders of what you would like to attract. In the process, they can help you make better decisions about your relationships, your finances, and your health.

- All crystals can help you feel rich. Surrounding yourself with glittering crystals and stones is one way to experience wealth, to get used to the sensation of owning beautiful things, and to start manifesting other material wealth, as well.

- All crystals, with their scintillating shimmer and shine, can even rub off on your personality—and help you feel brighter and more beautiful.

- All crystals can offer insight into your destiny. They all can serve as touchstones and reminders of the life you have lived so far . . . or other lives you've had in the past. Their connection to history can help you reflect on your past and plan for your future.

- All crystals—because they are so ancient—can help you recognize that life goes on, even in the face of crisis and change. In so doing, crystals can help you make both major and minor transitions more gracefully. As you move through those transitions, crystals can help you recognize cause and effect, be more conscious of your own actions, be more aware of your effect on other people, and be more aware of outside influences that are playing a role in your behavior and decision-making process. As a result, crystals can help you turn your experience into wisdom. Working with crystals can help you mature, develop your own innate leadership ability, and use your power wisely.

In short, all crystals are great healers and metaphysical tools. All you need to get started is to find the right crystals for you.

Getting Started

How to Use this Book

If you're reading this book, it's probably because something about crystals fascinates you. Maybe it's their beauty. Maybe it's how they feel in your hand. Maybe it's the sensations and impressions you get when you hold them, or maybe you simply like having them around because you know they're mystical . . . you're just not sure what you're supposed to *do* with them.

This book will give you practical advice and guidance on collecting crystals, understanding crystals, and working with crystals, whether you are a beginner or you have been admiring the shiny minerals for years.

Start by gathering whatever crystals, gemstones, and rocks you already have. With any luck, you may even have a few specimens from the "Top Twenty" recommended crystals in the next chapter. You can choose additional stones from the descriptions later in this guide.

One by one, you should learn to identify every crystal in your collection and get to know what each crystal in your collection has to offer you. You can use this book to read the brief description of each crystal, along with their properties and traditional associations and applications. You can also refer to a standard field guide to rocks and minerals.

You should also augment your reading with a guidebook of your own: simply start a notebook or journal to record your experiences along the way. It doesn't need to be particularly long or complicated endeavor. Simply date each entry, record which crystals you've worked with, and jot a few notes about your experiences. Over time, your crystals journal will become a virtual treasure chest of information about the gems and stones in your collection.

As you go, you'll not only learn what crystals can do in the hands of a skilled practitioner—you'll learn what crystals can do for you.

Starter Sets

The Top Twenty Crystals
for the Beginning User

If you don't have a crystal collection yet, start with the following "Top Twenty" recommended stones. They represent a broad cross-section of physical attributes and metaphysical properties, and they are all affordable and readily available.

1. **Agates** come in a wide variety of colors and appearances—striped, spotted, and variegated—but their distinctive bands of color hint at the layers and hidden depths inside us all. Each individual agate forms by filling a cavity in host rock. Agates were treasured during the Stone Age— they have been unearthed in archaeological digs of settlements in France that date back 22,000 years. The Egyptians used agate for jewelry and amulets 5,000 years ago. Persian magicians used agate to divert storms, and for a time, agates were believed to make their wearers invisible, quench thirst, and protect people from fevers. A hundred

years before Christ, Mithridates, the king of Pontus (in what is now Turkey), owned thousands of agate bowls.[1] Collecting agate bowls was also popular during the Byzantine Empire in the Middle Ages, as well as among European royalty during the Renaissance. The "Mystical Crystals" chapter has more information on specific types of agates.

2. Amethysts are regal, violet-colored stones. They are widely used by psychics, who find that amethysts' soothing energy gives their intuitive senses a boost. The ancient Romans believed that amethysts were inadvertently created by Bacchus, the Roman god of wine. According to legend, an ordinary mortal insulted Bacchus, so he created a team of tigers to destroy the next hapless mortal who crossed his path. Sadly, that mortal turned out to be a beautiful maiden named Amethyst. Diana, the goddess of the moon, was watching, and she did what she could to protect Amethyst—she turned her into a statue of pure quartz crystal, impervious to the tigers' claws. But when Bacchus saw how beautiful Amethyst had been, he regretted his foolish, poorly planned display of bad temper. He wept bitter tears of dark red wine over the crystal and stained it purple.[2]

Since then, amethyst has been known as the "sobriety stone." The ancients drank wine from amethyst goblets,

---

1. http://www.gemstone.org/gem-by-gem/english/agate.html

2. Alda Marian Jangl and James Francis Jangl, *Ancient Legends of Gems and Jewels* (Coeur d'Alene, ID: Primsa Press, 1985), 6.

believing the crystal would keep them from getting drunk. Even now, some people believe amethyst can help those who struggle with alcoholism, compulsive behaviors, and addictions of all kinds.

From the Egyptian pharaohs to the British royal family, amethysts have always been popular among royalty—in part because purple has always been thought of as a regal color. Leonardo da Vinci believed that amethyst could dispel evil thoughts and make people more intelligent. During the Middle Ages, Catholic church administrators believed that amethyst could not only help people stay sober, but that it could also help keep priests celibate. Amethysts eventually came to be regarded as the stone of bishops, and many bishops still wear amethyst rings to this day. In Tibet, Buddhists think of amethyst as a sacred stone and commonly craft rosaries from amethyst crystals.[3]

3. Aventurine is one of the loveliest crystals. Its soothing green color could almost be mistaken for jade, except for the fact that it contains small inclusions of several shiny minerals that give it a sparkling, glistening sheen. (The effect is known as *aventurescence*.) As its name implies, aventurine is a handy stone to have when you undertake any creative venture. It is also thought to be a particularly holistic, all-purpose healer, which helps with healing on spiritual, emotional, mental, and physical levels. Aventurine derived its name from a type of Italian glass. During the

---

3. http://www.gemstone.org/gem-by-gem/english/amethyst.html

eighteenth century, glass workers spilled copper filings into a batch of molten glass. The sparkling mixture, in Italian, was created *a ventura*—by chance.

4. Bloodstone, also known as heliotrope or warrior's stone, has been associated with health and well-being for centuries—primarily because of its color, a mesmerizing blend of dark red spots on a jade-green background. In ancient times, soldiers carried small pieces of bloodstone onto the battlefield as talismans to avoid injury and to stop bleeding.[4] Later, as Christianity swept the world, legend associated the stone with drops of Christ's blood that fell when he died on the cross. According to folklore, the stone was continually replenished by the blood of saints. One story even reports that a fourteenth-century gypsy once stole a bloodstone from Rome in order to give it to Romanian vampires as a peace offering; he apparently believed the legend that vampires could find an unending source of blood in the stone, so they wouldn't need to attack humans in order to survive.[5]

Not surprisingly, metaphysical healers have long used bloodstone to treat diseases of the blood and circulatory system, and to speed healing after surgery, ease menstrual cramps, and prevent miscarriage.

---

4. Scott Cunningham, *Cunningham's Encyclopedia of Crystal, Gem & Metal Magic* (St. Paul, MN: Llewellyn, 2004), 91.

5. http://wire-sculpture.com/Bloodstone.htm

5. Carnelian, a red, orange, or brown form of chalcedony, was traditionally sacred to Isis, the Egyptian goddess who revived her dead husband Osiris. For that reason, carnelian has come to symbolize all faithful wives and companions. The ancient Egyptians also believed that carnelian could ensure the soul's passage into the next world, and they filled their tombs with carnelian jewels. The prophet Mohammed was said to wear a carnelian ring on the little finger of his right hand.[6] Carnelian is also associated with eloquence and self-confidence; shy and timid people can boost their courage by wearing the stone.[7]

6. Citrine gets its name from the French word for lemon, *citron*. Citrine is simply yellow or orange quartz, but it is somewhat rare. Most of the citrine on the market is actually heat-treated amethyst or smoky quartz, but its yellow color lends it the same properties as genuine citrine. Like all yellow crystals, citrine is associated with the radiance and optimism of the sun. And like all gold-colored stones, citrine is associated with wealth and financial success.

7. Fluorite is also known as the genius stone. Whether you find a small sample or a large display piece of crystal, it won't be hard for you to imagine that you're looking at the skyline of New York or Chicago as the sun sets and twilight

---

6. George Frederick Kunz, *The Curious Lore of Precious Stones* (New York: Dover Publications, Inc., 1971), 64.

7. Cunningham, *Encyclopedia*, 94.

casts a blue and violet shadow on the entire city. On the other hand, if you're thinking on a smaller scale, fluorite's violet color and evenly spaced, gridlike formation could almost be mistaken for a high-tech computer component. Not surprisingly, fluorite is often associated with advanced civilization and high technology, and it can be a good crystal to have on hand if you do a lot of work with computers, or if you need to program yourself to think in more logical and rational terms. It's also no accident that "fluorite" sounds like "fluoride"—it is associated with dental health.

8. Hematite, a form of iron ore, is one of the best-known grounding stones. Its stabilizing energy can absorb and disburse negative thoughts and emotions. Hematite ranges in color from steel gray to deep, midnight black. Its reflective sheen makes it an ideal material for scrying, a form of divination in which people gaze into a reflective surface. Prehistoric men and women ground hematite to make red ochre pigment for their cave paintings. The ancient Egyptians used hematite for amulets, some of which were prescribed for madness and inflammation. Ancient Roman warriors associated hematite with Mars, the god of war, and they believed that if they rubbed hematite all over their bodies they would be invisible in battle. Pliny, the ancient Roman historian, also asserted that hematite would bring good luck to anyone who wore it while they petitioned the king or wanted a favorable judgment in a lawsuit. Even today, hematite is recommended for people facing tricky legal situations.

The word hematite comes from the Greek word *haema*, which means "blood." It refers to the red color found on unpolished specimens.

9. Howlite is a silky, snowy white stone with marble-like veins of gray or black. It's one of the most pleasing crystals to touch, because it feels like smooth, cool porcelain. Howlite is also one of the most intriguing stones to look at—most specimens are covered with a marbled web of black and grey streaks and veins. Its varied markings might encourage you to examine your own line of thought—especially regarding issues that seem to be black and white. While howlite was named after its discoverer, the Nova Scotia geologist Henry How, its spooky-sounding name also seems to connect it to the spirit world, and the stone may be one you'd like to use if you are trying to reach those who have crossed to the Other Side. (A side note: unscrupulous dealers sometimes dye howlite blue and try to pass it off as turquoise.)

10. Jasper comes in a rainbow of colors and designs, but it is commonly found in shades of red, brown, and orange. The various forms of jasper are usually named after their most distinctive characteristics. Landscape jasper, for example, seems to depict an entire landscape along its surface. Ribbon jasper seems to be wrapped in a ribbon. Poppy jasper seems to be covered with images of poppies. You can also choose from brecciated jasper, dalmatian jasper, king cobra jasper, leopard skin jasper, and more.

Jasper has been popular for centuries; there are records of jasper being used throughout the ancient world. In the fourth-century Greek poem "Lithica," jasper was called the great rain-bringer.[8]

Jasper might be the original touchstone. For thousands of years, people would rub gold-silver alloys on black jasper to test their gold content. The streak's color was a precise measure of gold content.

11. Lapis lazuli, the ancient alchemists' stone of heaven, does seem to reflect the skies above us. A dark blue crystal with flecks of golden pyrite, lapis lazuli was a sacred stone in Egypt. Some say the Ten Commandments were inscribed on tablets of lapis lazuli.[9] Egyptians used lapis for cosmetics and painting. Persians said that the heavens owed their blue color to a massive slab of lapis upon which the earth rested. And for centuries, painters have revered the blue pigment of crushed lapis lazuli.

12. Malachite, with its distinctive bands of light and dark green, is sometimes called the salesperson's stone because it can help buyers get bargains and it can help a salesperson close a deal. In ancient Egypt, people ground malachite into eye shadow. The Romans called it peacock stone and dedicated it to the goddess Juno.[10] During the Middle Ages, some used it as protection against black magic.

---

8. George Frederick Kunz, *The Curious Lore of Precious Stones* (New York: Dover Publications, 1971), 90.

9. Jangl and Jangl, *Ancient Legends*, 21.

10. Barbara G. Walker, *The Book of Sacred Stones* (New York: Harper-Collins, 1989), 147.

13. Moonstone embodies all of the magic and mystery we associate with the moon. The opalescent play of light that dances across the milky white surface of a moonstone is known as *adularescence*, and some people believe moonstones will grow brighter or dimmer along with the phases of the moon. Moonstone is also known as selenite, in honor of Selene, the Greek goddess of the moon. Moonstone was very popular with the Romans, who thought it was formed out of moonlight; it was used in Roman jewelry for centuries. In India, moonstone is still considered a sacred stone.

14. Obsidian is a rich, black volcanic glass, like a tinted window into the soul. Because it is so black and so heavy, many people believe obsidian is the most grounding stone available. Prehistoric people used obsidian to craft jewelry and tools; examples have been carbon dated to about 21000 BC. Today, obsidian is commonly used for scrying. You can choose from regular black obsidian, white-patterned snowflake obsidian, or legendary Apache tears.

15. Peridot, a gem born in fire, is found both in volcanic rocks and meteors. Because it is a form of olivine, peridot is always green. It is sometimes known as chrysolite, which means "golden stone" in Greek.

People have valued peridot for centuries. The Egyptians prized it and called it the gem of the sun. (Some of Cleopatra's emeralds were actually peridots.) The ancient Romans wore it to protect themselves from enchantments. Pliny, the ancient historian, mentioned a deposit on Saint John's Island in the Red Sea that still produces gems. During the Middle Ages, people wore peridot to gain foresight and divine inspiration. Some people even believed that peridot could drive away evil and cast out demons.

16. Petrified wood has an inherent link to the past. It is a tangible reminder of ancient ways and ancient knowledge, as well as a physical connection to the ongoing world of nature. Obviously, petrified wood can help you connect to the world of trees and plants. It can also teach you about preservation and survival. Some people use petrified wood as a tool for past-life regression by holding it and studying it during meditation.

Petrified wood is one of those odd crystals that didn't originate inside the earth—it was organic once. Petrified wood is a type of fossil in which the tissues of a dead plant are replaced with minerals. The petrification process occurs underground, after wood or woody materials suddenly become buried under sediment. Mineral-rich water flows through the sediment, depositing minerals in the plant's cells. As the original plant decays, a detailed stone cast is left in its place.

If you like working with petrified wood, you might also consider looking for amber, which is petrified tree sap. In many cases, amber crystals include the fossilized remains of small insects that crawled and buzzed around the earth's surface millions of years ago.

17. Quartz. As you start to work with crystals, you should have no trouble finding quartz for your collection—quartz is the second most common mineral in the earth's crust, after feldspar.

In ancient times, people believed that rock crystal was actually a form of ice. The Greeks thought of quartz as the ice of eternity; the word *crystallos* means "frozen." Mystics have called it the "philosopher's stone." Even modern scientists, who generally refer to quartz as silicon dioxide, are impressed with its physical and chemical properties: quartz can store, send, and receive energy, both physically and metaphysically.

Quartz comes in countless varieties. Even crystals known by other names, when it comes right down to it, are quartz. It would be entirely possible to put together an extensive collection of crystals consisting only of quartz.

Pure quartz, composed of silicon dioxide, is colorless and transparent—but when a tiny portion of the silicon atoms are replaced with iron, aluminum, manganese, or titanium, the crystal can take on beautiful colors. Amethyst is violet quartz. Jasper is quartz with red, yellow, brown, gray, or black coloring. Onyx and agate are quartz with bands of color. Bloodstone is green quartz with red spots.

If you are just beginning your work with crystals, start with clear quartz. It's probably the most versatile crystal. You can use clear quartz for any metaphysical purpose, including meditation, divination, dream work, and healing. As soon as you can, add soothing rose quartz and cleansing smoky quartz to your collection, too.

More information on specific types of quartz can be found in the "Mystical Crystals" chapter.

18. Rhodonite gets its name from *rhodon*, the Greek word for rose. It is a stone of contrasts—it is both hot pink, which represents passion, and a grounded, deep, rich black. In eighteenth-century Russia, decorators used rhodonite throughout the royal court. Rhodonite is sometimes called the singer's stone, and it is often associated with the throat chakra.

19. Sodalite, the student's stone, is a dark blue stone with white bands. Its crisp, contrasting colors are clean and refreshing. Sodalite can help you focus, concentrate, remember, learn, and organize your knowledge. Some people keep sodalite near their computers and television sets to absorb electromagnetic emissions.

20. Tiger's eye is a brown chalcedony with gold highlights. When tiger's eye is cut and polished, it reveals *chatoyancy*— a narrow band of white light that looks like the eye of a tiger. Ancient Romans carried tiger's eye into battle, believing that it would speed up their reaction time. You might also like to collect a specimen or two of hawk's eye, which is a midnight blue version of tiger's eye.

The Treasure Hunt

Collecting Crystals

You can find crystals in stone and gem stores, metaphysical shops, and gift shops. Crystals are so popular that you can come across them in bookstores, discount outlets, and drug stores. Sometimes you can even find them in places you wouldn't expect, like supermarkets and truck stops.

You don't necessarily have to search high and low for your crystals. If a crystal is meant to come to you, you might discover that it will make its way to your door without your help.

You could also find yourself stumbling across some varieties of stones and crystals in your own backyard. Look around—crystals in their raw form, discovered in their natural environment, have an innate power that's hard to resist. You might even want to start your search for stones and crystals on the way *to* your local rock shop, rather than inside it.

Smart Shopping

While you may be interested in using crystals for New Age purposes like meditation, healing, and psychic development, you've also got something in common with geologists, gemologists, rock collectors, and jewelers—people who collect crystals as objects of beauty, value, and scientific fascination.

As you start assembling your crystal collection, you can borrow some of their criteria to help you be a smart shopper. Here are some terms and concepts that you should know when you shop for crystals:

Color. Jewelers and gemologists say that color is the most important factor in determining the value of a gemstone—at least when it comes to jewelry. Most dealers say that color accounts for 50 to 70 percent of a stone's value.

Color is also an important metaphysical consideration. Bright, pure colors are usually best. Technically speaking, the most powerful crystals don't look washed out in bright sunlight, and they don't look too dark in ordinary room light. As you shop, you should pay attention to how the crystals look under varying light conditions, including natural and artificial light.

Hue. The term *hue* simply refers to color. The human eye can distinguish 150 different hues, including all the colors of the rainbow: red, orange, yellow, green, blue, indigo, and violet.

Tone. The relative lightness or darkness of a hue is known as *tone*. Gemologists rate tone on a scale that ranges from colorless (0) to black (10).

Saturation. Saturation refers to the purity of a color. Crystals that have a lot of gray or brown are less saturated with other, brighter colors, and they look dull as a result. Likewise, crystals that are too light are also poorly saturated, because they look washed out. Saturation is measured on a scale that ranges from neutral (0) to vivid (6).

Transparency. Transparency describes how well light passes through a crystal. There are three degrees of transparency. *Transparent* crystals, like clear quartz, are as clear as window glass. *Translucent* crystals, like amethyst, will allow light to pass through, but you can't see objects through them. *Opaque* crystals, like hematite, don't allow any light to pass through. You can't see anything through an opaque crystal.

Luster. Luster is shine—the way the surface of a mineral reflects light. For the most part, the terms used to describe luster are self-explanatory: metallic or nonmetallic, dull, earthy, fibrous, greasy, pearly, silky, and waxy.

Clarity. Few crystals are perfectly clear. Most have *inclusions*—particles of foreign matter, such as dirt, dust, other minerals, or even pockets of water or oil. Inclusions can actually add to a crystal's usefulness and value, depending on the stone.

Size. Generally speaking, crystals are measured by weight (in carats) or by size, in either inches or millimeters.

- Most precious gems, especially those used in jewelry-making, are weighed in carats. The word *carat* is derived from the word *carob*, and it hearkens back to the days when ancient Mediterranean jewelers and stonecutters would use carob seeds to balance their scales. One carat is equal to ⅕ of a gram, which is about the weight of a carob seed.

- Other crystal specimens are commonly measured in millimeters, either in circumference or diameter.

- Raw crystals can also be sold by the piece, by weight, or by flat, table, or lot.

Grade. Grading systems may vary from dealer to dealer, and would generally be of most importance to serious mineralogists, gemologists, and jewelers. However, you might see some crystals graded by letter or number. As a rule, AAA-rated crystals are practically flawless, with no chips, fractures, or inclusions. AA-rated crystals would be slightly flawed, with small marks, inclusions, or fractures that don't affect more than 10 percent of the stone. The ratings go down proportionately; seriously flawed, damaged, or included stones might rate only a C or a D.

Enhanced and treated crystals. Many crystals are enhanced and treated, both to boost their appearance and to ensure that they can be handled and used in daily life. Some crystals are bleached, for example. Others may be dyed or treated with heat or radiation to change their color. A reputable dealer will tell you if a crystal has been changed in any way.

Spotted or Striped

The term "crystal" isn't always as precise or accurate as you might think. A wide range of objects fall loosely into the crystals category, and most crystal shops carry a wide selection of crystals that aren't really crystals at all.

By definition, crystals are minerals—inorganic elements, usually in solid form, that occur naturally. Most minerals are composed of a single chemical element, or a mixture of closely related chemicals. And most minerals are symmetrical—they grow in precisely angled geometric patterns, and they have a repetitive crystalline structure that reflects the internal arrangement of their atoms.

In everyday terms, however, some "crystals" are actually rocks, aggregates, organic materials, and even metals.

Rocks. Rocks are a conglomerate of many minerals, chemicals, and solid organic materials that come from inside the earth. In other words, rocks are a mix of elements that have cemented, fused, or bonded together. Granite, marble, and lapis lazuli, for example, are all rocks.

Aggregates. Some crystals are also aggregates, which consist of thousands of microscopic crystals. Chalcedony crystals, which include agates and jaspers, are aggregates of quartz.

You can work with rocks and aggregates just as easily as you can work with "pure" crystals. Some people believe that their power is less focused or more dispersed because they're not a single type of crystal. However, one could also argue that there is power in numbers, and that rocks and aggregates are a tangible reminder of the power of sticking together, working in partnership with others, and acting as part of a community.

Organics. Some crystals are organic materials, like pearl, coral, and amber. They don't originate deep within the earth; they come from living beings that once lived on the earth's surface. They still are called crystals because they share many of the same qualities and features as their mineral counterparts—they are smooth, symmetrical, and polished, and they are valued for their beauty, their history, and their symbolism.

Stones. Gemstones—or stones, for short—are usually crystals that can be cut and polished for jewelry. While almost any mineral can be cut like a gemstone, not all crystals are gemstones. In order to qualify, they must be beautiful, durable, and rare. And likewise, not all gemstones are crystals, because some lack a definite crystalline structure. Amber, for example, is fossilized tree resin. Jet is compacted coal, obsidian is volcanic glass, and opals are hydrated silica.

Traditionally, gemstones have been divided into two categories: precious and semiprecious. The terms have become so overused, though, that they don't mean much anymore. Diamonds are always precious gems, for example, but some diamonds can be fairly inexpensive, and some semiprecious stones are incredibly expensive.

Elements of Attraction

Here are some ways to go about finding the crystals you'll want in your collection:

Tune in. Before you start your search or shopping expedition, relax. Take some deep breaths. Calm and center yourself. Try to clear your mind of clutter.

If you are looking for a crystal to help you with a specific issue, think of it, or even write it down in your crystals journal before you leave the house. Clearly state your intention and the universe will be more likely to provide it for you.

If you don't have anything specific in mind, however, and you'd like to stay open to any crystals that might be waiting for you, simply look around and be receptive to the impressions you get from holding or looking at the crystals.

Symbolic significance. You can familiarize yourself with the traditional significance and customary attributes of crystals and make your selection accordingly. This guide is a good starting point; other books on the market, like Scott Cunningham's *Encyclopedia of Crystal, Gem & Metal Magic,* can give you more detailed descriptions of popular stones.

Physical attraction. There is nothing wrong with choosing crystals that are strikingly beautiful or crystals that seem to scintillate, sparkle, and shine. Physical beauty is the reason most people are attracted to crystals in the first place. You should know, however, that some of your most powerful, most usable crystals might not strike you as attractive—at least, not in the usual sense of the word. Crystals that are chipped, broken, cloudy, or otherwise marred may have metaphysical properties that you need and want in your collection. So while you can choose crystals based on how they look, remember that real beauty also lies in the eye of the beholder.

Size. You might want to concentrate on collecting crystals of a certain size so you can keep your entire collection together. You might want to start your collection by choosing only crystals that fit in the palm of your hand or small, pocket-size stones that you can wear or carry wherever you go. You might want to position your entire collection on a bookshelf, a coffee table, or a tabletop. A crystal's power is unrelated to its size, so you can set any parameters you like for your collection.

Intuition. You might feel especially drawn to some crystals but not others. Pay attention to your intuition: do you feel some stones that seem to be calling to you? When you're in a store, do you feel compelled to look down one particular aisle, or one corner of the shop? Go there first.

Occasionally, you might feel drawn to a crystal without knowing the reason why. If you can afford the crystal, buy it. It may sit in your collection for years, but one day, its significance will suddenly be obvious—or someday, you may suddenly feel compelled to give it to someone else, and you'll realize that your role was simply to safeguard the crystal until you could deliver it to its rightful owner.

Good vibrations. If you are choosing crystals from a large bin or a box—as with tumbled stones—you can simply reach in, feel around, and choose the stone that feels best in your hand. Alternately, if you are choosing a crystal from an array of stones in front of you, try rubbing your hands briskly together to warm them up. Then hold your left hand (which is your intuitive hand, if you're right-handed) over the stone. (Conversely, use your right hand if you're left-handed.) When you find the right crystal, you might feel a tingling sensation, a magnetic attraction, an electrical charge, or a temperature change. You could also hold a crystal in both hands and point it toward your heart or hold it over the third-eye chakra on the middle of your forehead to see if you are moved to add it to your collection.

Can't feel the vibe? Practice feeling your own energy first. Rub your hands together briskly. Hold them close together, palms facing in, and then gradually pull them apart. Experiment with moving your hands together and apart until you can feel the energy between them.

Pendulum dowsing. You might enjoy dowsing for your next crystal. Use a small pendulum—available from any

New Age shop—suspended from a chain. Use your thumb and index finger to hold the chain.

First, determine how you should interpret your pendulum's movements. Ask the pendulum to show you "yes." It will probably swing in a definite pattern, side to side, for example, or back and forth. Then ask the pendulum to show you "no." You should be able to see a distinct difference in movement.

Once you are comfortable with how your pendulum works, hold it over any crystals you are considering, and ask which ones you should buy.

Wait for crystals to come to you. As you begin your work with crystals, let others know about your new pursuit. When your friends and family members learn that you're interested in crystals, you might find yourself with more crystals, rocks, and gemstones than you know what to do with. Crystals that are used for metaphysical purposes also tend to get passed around to whomever needs them. They circulate from friend to friend, and they travel where they are needed most. Ultimately, because all crystals are ancient, they pause only briefly in the life of any one person.

The Inside Story

The Origins of Crystals, Rocks, and Stones

More than five billion years ago, a star exploded in a fiery supernova, and our solar system was born.

That initial explosion was massive. It spewed an almost unimaginable amount of wreckage into a nearby cloud of hydrogen gas and interstellar dust. The cosmic debris began to spin, and at the center, a new star—our sun—began to form.

All around that nascent sun, the matter in the swirling disk also began to collide and clump together; bits of iron, silicon, magnesium, aluminum, and oxygen met and combined. Over millions of years, the collisions produced larger and larger bodies in space. The larger they grew, the harder they hit. As they collided, they exploded, and their components began to separate and sort themselves out. As dense iron settled in the center, and lighter rock separated into a mantle around the iron core, the planets we know and recognize today began to take shape.

Then suddenly, the sun ignited. The force of that explosion blew away the hydrogen gas in the cloud, and only the planets remained.

At that point, the earth was an ocean of red-hot molten rock. As the collisions slowed down, our planet began to cool. Its surface crusted over, but inside its core, the molten magma continued to boil and bubble. Periodically, water vapor broke through the crust and condensed in the earth's atmosphere. Clouds formed. Rain fell and fed primordial oceans.

And crystals formed.

In fact, when you hold a crystal in your hand, you could very well be holding an object as old as the universe itself.

Many people are attracted to crystals simply because they are so old. That fact makes them fascinating to contemplate. They were here eons before humankind, and they will last far longer than any of us. In fact, the oldest rocks found on earth are almost four billion years old.

The earth itself might be considered a giant rock. Its center, as you probably learned in grade school, is surrounded by pure liquid rock—molten magma, 1,860 miles thick.

Most crystals spring from the center of the earth. The earth's center is surrounded by a crust of massive plates that range from three miles to twenty-five miles thick. Most of the crust is covered by ocean water, while we live on massive, continental islands of granite, floating on the mantle of the earth.

It can be a bumpy ride. As the magma in the earth's core roils and boils, the continental plates shift, rub, and occasionally crash into each other. In the process, some areas of the world erupt in volcanoes, while other areas tremble their way through earthquakes. Some parts of the earth are thrust down, back toward the core, while others rise up in the form of mountain ranges and vast plains of lava.

As the earth's crust shifts, it fractures, creating fissures and cavities. Chemical-rich fluids flow through the newly created spaces. And suddenly, all of the ingredients for crystal creation are in place—chemical components, trapped under high pressure, with time to grow.

Crystals form when chemicals, heat, pressure, time, and space combine in just the right measure. Crystals are seeded when liquids cool or freeze into solids, when dissolved matter precipitates out of a solution or gases condense. Exactly what types of crystals will form depends on the chemical mix in play, as well as the time, temperature, and pressure involved.

Some crystals, like diamonds, emeralds, and rubies, form deep within the earth, as molten rock cools slowly over long periods of time. Some crystals grow inside gas bubbles, after magma has reached the surface. Others form as water and other liquids evaporate. However, simply having molten rock available is no guarantee that crystals will form. If molten rock cools too quickly—as when lava is ejected from a volcano—there won't be time for crystals to take shape. And if some of the conditions aren't just right, some chemical elements will simply cool into aggregates of small interlocking crystals.

Even when all of the correct elements are at hand for crystal creation, fissures and openings deep within the earth can close, which can shut some crystals off from their source of chemical nutrients. They stop growing as a result. Also as the earth's crust shifts, crystals can break. New elements can be introduced into the mix, which can affect a crystal's chemical makeup, color, and growth patterns. Sometimes, chemical impurities can crystallize inside a host, or cavities of gas can be incorporated within a crystal.

Ultimately, there are three ways that crystals can be created:

- **Igneous rocks and crystals** form deep within the earth, when red-hot magma cools. It could cool beneath the surface of the earth, or it could erupt in a volcano and cool on the surface. Igneous rocks that cooled slowly are usually comprised of large grains of minerals because each grain had more time to grow. Igneous rocks that cooled quickly are finer and look more delicate.

- **Metamorphic rocks and crystals** form when the earth buckles and shifts, which puts some crystals under intense pressure or high temperatures. Some crystals melt when they are exposed to heat, or when they come into direct contact with hot magma that has forced its way into cracks and fissures. Some minerals can also be transformed into other minerals without melting first. They may undergo a chemical shift as a result of heat and pressure, or they could come into contact with chemical solutions that migrate through the rocks. They might even be forced to combine with other minerals by being squeezed into the same place at the same time.

- **Sedimentary rocks and crystals** form as minerals crystallize from layers of sediment in low-temperature solutions. That sediment generally comes from igneous rocks worn away by rivers and streams. Bit by bit, piece by piece, flowing water carries those rocks and crystals away and washes them into lakes, oceans, or seas. Over time, those fragments are laid down in layers, where they harden into rock.

The cycle can be repetitive—sedimentary rocks can be transformed into metamorphic rocks, or they can be shaken loose during earthquakes, tumble back toward the earth's core, and melt once more into magma. From cooling magma, crystals form. With time and heat and pressure, they undergo metamorphosis. Once exposed to the elements, they can tumble free or be worn and washed away into sedimentary deposits . . . where once again they can find themselves reborn in the center of the earth.

How Quartz Crystals Grow

Because quartz is the most common crystal on earth and it's the mainstay of many crystal collections, it's especially interesting to note how quartz crystals form.

Quartz consists of silicon and oxygen, the two most common chemical elements in the earth's crust. You can find quartz in igneous, metamorphic, and sedimentary rocks. Quartz is an integral component of granite and sandstone, and most grains of sand are actually weathered fragments of quartz. It isn't strictly limited to earth's surface, either; scientists have found quartz in meteorites and moon rocks.

Most quartz crystals start as a hot, vaporous, supersaturated solution of silicon dioxide. As the hot liquids and gases inside the earth begin to cool, they also begin to condense. As they move from the ethereal to a solid, physical existence, a few single seed cells set the stage for everything still to come. A single molecule of four oxygen atoms and one silicon atom links together and bonds to a *matrix*—a base or foundation rock, like granite or sandstone. As time passes, more atoms group together, and more molecules adhere to that base. Millions of atoms link together in a network or pattern called a *lattice*, and the quartz crystals continue to grow, layer after layer, in a spiraling, six-sided solid that reflects the hexagonal structure of the molecules themselves.

Crystals

*The Flowers of the
Mineral Kingdom*

When you hold a perfect crystal, you can literally see its atomic structure. However, perfect crystals—like perfect people—are rare.

Crystals usually crystallize into one of seven geometric forms: triangles, squares, rectangles, hexagons, rhomboids, parallelograms, or trapeziums.

- **Triangles**. Crystals with three perfect sides are *trigonal* crystals.

- **Squares**. Crystals with four equal sides, like a cube, are *isometric* crystals.

- **Rectangles**. Crystals shaped like long, tall rectangles are *tetragonal* crystals.

- **Hexagons**. Crystals with six sides are *hexagonal* crystals.

- **Rhomboids**. Crystals shaped like short, wide rectangles are *orthorhombic* crystals.

- **Parallelograms.** Crystals that are short and stubby with tilted faces at each end are *monoclinic* crystals.
- **Trapeziums.** Crystals that look like pyramids with their tops cut off are trapeziums.

Don't Judge a Crystal by Its Cover

You can't always tell what kind of crystal you hold in your hand just based on its appearance. Mineralogists who want to identify a crystal typically have to test a number of physical properties, including color, streak, transparency, luster, hardness, cleavage, fracture, specific gravity, and crystal form.

Color. Color can be a crystal's most obvious property, but it is an unreliable tool for determining what type of crystal you're looking at. Some minerals are always the same color—but don't count on it. Just a trace element of another mineral can change its color completely. Quartz, for example, comes in every hue.

Streak. If you rub a crystal firmly across an unglazed white porcelain tile, it will leave a streak—a powdery line. Every type of crystal will always leave the same streak, even if individual specimens have impurities.

Hardness. In 1812, a German mineralogist named Fredrich Mohs devised the Mohs scale of mineral hardness. That scale is now the universal measure of mineral hardness: talc is the softest mineral, followed by gypsum, calcite, fluorite, apatite, feldspar, quartz, topaz, corundum, and diamond.

Cleavage. If you were to hit a mineral sample with a hammer, it would break along the weakest planes of its crystalline structure—its cleavages. Some minerals break in one direction, while others break in two or more directions. Some minerals cleave perfectly in one direction but poorly in others. Cleavage can be an important clue to a crystal's identity.

Fracture. Not all minerals cleave easily. Some fracture instead. Unlike cleavages—which are usually clean, flat breaks—fractures can be smoothly curved, irregular, uneven, jagged, or splintery.

Specific gravity is calculated by comparing a crystal's weight to the weight of an equal volume of water. Heavier minerals have a greater specific gravity.

The Science
and the Superstition

How Crystals Work

For centuries, people have used crystals for both practical purposes—from flint fire starters to butane lighters—as well as for metaphysical endeavors like healing, meditation, and psychic communication. And while our civilization has advanced, our quest for spiritual fulfillment is as primal as ever.

How can crystals be so much a part of our ordinary lives and still rise to the level of the extraordinary? How can something we routinely take for granted also make it possible for us to reach new levels of consciousness? How do crystals really work?

To understand the metaphysics behind the physics, it doesn't hurt to take a quick survey of the science and the symbolism associated with crystals.

Scientific Properties

Crystals have several consistent and predictable scientific properties, and most people who use them for spiritual work believe those scientific properties have a symbolic counterpart in the metaphysical universe, too.

- Crystals are *piezoelectric*. In other words, when crystals are squeezed, they generate electricity, and when electricity passes through them, they change shape.

- Crystals are also *pyroelectric*, which means they can produce electricity as a result of temperature changes.

- And crystals have *resonance*, which means that they will vibrate in response to other frequencies in their area.

In the last hundred years or so, crystals have played a lead role in the development of entertainment and communication technology. Because crystals can change electrical vibrations into sound waves and broadcast signals, they were an integral component of early sound recordings, as well as radio and television broadcasting. And because crystals vibrate at a precise rate, they have also become an essential tool for accurately marking the passage of time—not only in quartz clocks and watches, as you might expect, but also in radio transmitters, radio receivers, and computers.

In fact, the scientific properties of crystals were instrumental in the development of today's high-tech devices like sonar, laser beams, and atomic microscopes. It's no coincidence that quartz crystals are made up of silicon dioxide, and the world's most famous computer hub is known as Silicon Valley.

All told, crystals can perform a number of functions—in both the physical and the spiritual world.

- Crystals can receive energy.

- Crystals can store energy.

- Crystals can release energy.

- Crystals can reflect, refract, and magnify energy.

- Crystals can transform energy.

- Crystals can balance and harmonize energy.

- Crystals can organize energy.

- Crystals can tune in to energy from other sources.

- Crystals can make it possible for us to observe and perceive that energy.

- Crystals can amplify, focus, and redirect energy.

- Crystals can be used as communication devices because their energy patterns transmit signals.

- Crystals can be used to record the passage of time and events.

There is practically no end to the scientific properties and uses of crystals.

To clearly understand some of a crystal's scientific properties—and their corresponding metaphysical uses—picture an old-fashioned land-line telephone. When you talk, the sound of your voice vibrates a crystal. That vibration generates an electrical pattern in the crystal. In essence, sound is converted to electricity. At the other end of the line, the electrical pattern of your voice is received by another crystal, which generates a replica of the sound of your voice.

That's basically how radio and traditional television signals are transmitted through the air, too. A crystal can generate signals at one location, and then transmit them to other crystals in other receiving stations.

You can literally put an electrical pattern into a crystal. You can program crystals to receive information, convert it to electricity, transmit that electricity, and duplicate that information in another location. Whatever you put in, you get back out.

It might make you wonder: if you can program a crystal to help you talk to your brother in Boise, why couldn't you program a crystal to communicate with your grandmother in the afterworld? If crystals can do so much for science and technology, why couldn't they be equally effective in the metaphysical world?

Quantum Physics

While some scientists will immediately disparage metaphysical use of crystals as pseudoscience, the two worldviews might not be as far apart as you think. In fact, both physics and metaphysics could fit comfortably under the umbrella of quantum physics.

Think of it this way: on one hand, we have metaphysics. For thousands of years, spiritualists, mystics, and seekers have taught that our waking world was only an illusion, while reality was somewhere else—somewhere far apart from the hustle and bustle of physical existence. The world we know, they say, is merely a shadow or reflection of the real world. Even today, the idea that spiritual reality is somehow removed from material reality is a mainstay of many metaphysical systems.

On the other hand, we have modern science. In 1514, Nicolaus Copernicus put the sun—and not Earth—at the center of the universe. Before long, science replaced superstition, and Western thinkers started to base all of their studies on the assumption that the natural world is a completely logical and objective place. In our world of Newtonian physics and Darwinian evolution, life unfolds, one event after another, in an inescapably linear progression of cause and effect. Every occurrence—even those we can't explain—somehow conforms to the laws of nature.

Now, through the study of quantum physics, it seems that both schools of thought could be correct; even according to the laws of nature, a subjective and an objective world could coexist.

Crystals offer a window into that dual reality.

While crystals seem solid, modern physicists have demonstrated that physical objects consist of energy, not matter. Crystals are highly structured units of energy. On a quantum level, crystals, like everything else, are in constant motion, dancing to the vibrations of the universe.

The laws of nature are imprinted in the patterns and structure of a crystal. Crystals are made of elements. Each element always has the same fixed number of protons and electrons. The way those elements are organized at a molecular and atomic level determines what shape and form each crystal will take. In other words, structure at the quantum level determines which reality will appear.

The structure of a crystal also affects its ability to send and receive energy in the form of electrons and protons, or electromagnetic waves. Unfortunately, that has proven to be something of a puzzle for modern science, because when physicists start to study crystals on a quantum level, some odd developments start to occur.

For one thing, scientists have found that the signal between two crystals travels at the speed of light. While the speed of light is fast, it's not instantaneous. In theory, scientists should be able to pinpoint the location of electrons and protons as they move from one crystal to another.

In practice, however, electrons and protons at the quantum level seem to travel *faster* than the speed of light. They don't even travel in the sense that scientists expect. Instead, they embody a certain timelessness, and they seem to be everywhere at once.

That means that sometimes there is no set starting point for the transmission of energy—and there's no middle or end point, either. When scientists study the communication between two crystals, the only thing they can establish is that there is some exchange of energy between the two.

At that point, scientists can be hard-pressed to discern the difference between the transmitter crystal and the receiver.

Logically, that doesn't make sense—especially if you're used to thinking in terms of linear time, with a beginning, a middle, and an end to a transmission. The problem is compounded by the fact that the receiver seems to affect the transmitter, even before communication begins.

Ultimately, that's the real problem. Apparently, time is not linear—at least, not on a quantum level. Instead, time as we know it is hardly a physical property at all. Some might even conclude that time is simply a trick of the mind.

It's a good trick; our understanding of time helps us make sense of the world. Our ideas about time help us recognize cause and effect, and make it possible for us to single out connections and study their patterns. Unfortunately, our awareness of time might also keep us from comprehending the depth and scope of the universe as a whole.

According to quantum physics, while we think we're watching reality unfold, we are actually observing just one version of reality—a series of snapshots, really—isolated from an infinite number of other possibilities that continue to run their course in the rest of the universe.

It's true that two crystals that send and receive energy are connected in a linear structure. One crystal really does send information while another receives it. But that one connection might not be the only connection between the two. According to quantum theory, there are countless connections between those crystals and between everything else in the universe. Those countless connections cross and crisscross as they spiral and weave across the universe. While they affect the reality we can see, we simply can't observe them without isolating them, too.

Ultimately, the study of quantum physics might do more than simply explain how crystals can send and receive information in the physical world. If time really is only a matter of perspective and all things are connected on a subatomic level, then quantum physics might also explain how psychic phenomena fits into the big picture. Quantum physics could explain how crystals can store or reflect metaphysical information like thoughts, feelings, and memories—just what you might expect to see when you gaze into a crystal ball—and quantum physics could explain how related fields like astrology, tarot, and runes work, too.

Structural Integrity

You don't have to master electronic engineering or quantum physics to see how crystals might have an effect on humans. You only need to look down at your arms and legs.

People have a lot in common with crystals. You could even say that human beings are walking, talking, crystal radio receivers and transmitters, attuned not only to each other, but also to the energy of the physical world around us.

While crystals are composed of atoms, linked together in a perfectly symmetrical, spiraling design, we humans have a crystalline structure of our own. From the spiraling double helix of our DNA to the highly organized, symmetrical design of our bones, muscles, and skin, we might actually be thought of as living, breathing crystals.

We even share two essential components with crystals: silicon and oxygen, the two most common components of the earth's crust. Our DNA is shaped like a spiral lattice, like a crystal. And because we are made up of atoms, which are mostly space and wave particles, we are really vibrating waves of light and energy.

Just like crystals, our bodies have the ability to gather, store, and release energy. We can also reflect, refract, and magnify that energy. We can balance and harmonize energy within ourselves. We can tune in to energy from other sources; amplify, focus, and redirect that energy; and we can achieve remarkable transformations, even if we don't always act in predictable, scientific ways.

The Power of Intention

You might not feel like it when you're stuck in a traffic jam or when your neighbors start their lawn mower at 7 a.m., but we are all spiritual beings in physical form. Crystals might work simply because they remind us of our unique place in the universe and because they help us balance the spiritual and material realms of our existence.

Crystals may be the ultimate physical beings. They are more structured, more systematic, and more logically organized than practically any other object in the natural world. And yet, they seem to reflect a spiritual existence. They literally look like spirit in physical form. When you hold a crystal, it's not hard to imagine that the light and energy of the heavens has somehow materialized in the palm of your hand.

Crystals give form to our imagination. They reflect the shape of our own thoughts, and they remind us that physical existence can be beautiful.

On a very fundamental level, a crystal can be a physical manifestation of your most heartfelt hopes, dreams, and wishes, and a crystal can serve as a tangible reminder of your goals and highest ideals.

The Elemental Array

The ancient Greeks believed that the world was composed of four elements: earth, water, air, and fire. They found those elements everywhere they looked—in the natural world, the philosophical world, and in their own physical and spiritual lives.

Since the ancient Greeks first developed their worldview, metaphysical thinkers have come to associate the four elements with the four aspects of human life: the fiery passion of spiritual concerns, the fluid, watery world of emotional affairs, the airy atmospheric awareness of intellectual life, and the earthly realities of physical existence.

Crystals embody all four elements at once. They are born of earth and fire, but their beauty can only surface when they are exposed to air and they begin to reflect and transform the light around them. And, as you know, their very name reflects their connection to water: *crystallos* is Greek for "frozen."

Sacred Geometry

For some people, crystals seem to work because they serve as a tangible reminder that the universe is an orderly place, designed and run by an intelligent creator.

Euclid, the ancient Greek mathematician now considered to be the father of geometry, once wrote, "The laws of nature are but the mathematical thoughts of God."

Crystals always grow according to an orderly, systematic design. In fact, all of nature follows strict mathematical formulas. Once scientists and philosophers follow those formulas to their ultimate conclusions, they find themselves in the realm of sacred geometry—a branch of thought in which mathematics starts to look like the language of God. Crystals have long served as evidence of sacred geometry, and they also serve as models for higher, more refined discoveries.

Long ago, in ancient Greece, an entire school of learning was once devoted to studying and understanding five simple shapes: the Platonic Solids. Today, those forms still stand unparalleled as models for advanced thought.

At first glance, the Platonic Solids seem plain, even ordinary. That's probably because we see them everywhere, in nature and in man-made objects alike. When it comes right down to it, the Platonic Solids are all just simple triangles and squares—but each one is a clue in understanding the natural world. Each one, coincidentally enough, also happens to show up in the physical structure of crystals.

- **The tetrahedron**, or triangular pyramid, has four sides. Each side is a perfect equilateral triangle.

- **The hexahedron**, or cube, has six sides. Each side is a perfect square.

- **The octahedron** has eight sides. Each side is a perfect equilateral triangle.

- **The dodecahedron** has twelve sides. Each side is a perfect five-sided pentagon.

- **The icosahedron** has twenty sides. Each side is a perfect equilateral triangle.

Geometrically speaking, the five Platonic Solids are intriguing to look at—and fun to think about.

- Each one has the same shape on all of its sides.
- Each side is exactly the same length.
- Every angle on a facet is identical.
- Every Platonic Solid will fit perfectly inside a sphere, and their outside corners will all touch the edges of the sphere.

The ancient Greeks were fascinated by the Platonic Solids. They even speculated that the five Platonic Solids constituted the fundamental shapes of the physical universe. What's more, they determined that the Platonic solids symbolized earth, water, fire, air, and spirit—the building blocks not only of the world, but also of human experience.

Symbolism, Synchronicity, and the Collective Unconscious

Crystals have been used for so many years, by so many people, that there is quite a body of history, legendary associations, and symbolism associated with most crystals.

Everyone knows, for example, that diamonds symbolize everlasting love. Red rubies and garnets symbolize passion. For centuries, sailors and travelers have carried ocean-blue aquamarines to ensure safe and speedy voyages.

It may be that when you tap into the power of crystals, you also tap into the power of the myths and legends associated with them.

You don't even need to be conscious of those myths and legends to feel their effect in your life. If you believe in synchronicity, Carl Jung's theory of meaningful coincidence, you might find yourself working with just the right crystal at just the right time, without being aware of its symbolic significance and meaning.

Life is filled with surprising twists and turns of fate—you might think of a long-lost friend, for example, only to meet him on the street the next day. You might get a craving for roast beef, and then discover that it's the dinner special at your favorite restaurant. Your flight might get cancelled at the last minute, but on the next plane out you find yourself seated next to the woman who will someday become your wife.

Famed psychiatrist Carl Jung developed the theory of synchronicity to explain all of those meaningful coincidences. Jung believed that some chance encounters—like finding the right crystal at the right time—aren't actually chance at all. Instead, he argued, they are the sign of a higher power at work and an intelligent design in the universe.

Jung suggested that we all are a part of that design, with the ability to tap into the collective unconscious for information and guidance in our daily lives. The collective unconscious, he explained, is the bond of shared emotion and understanding that unites all people on a psychic level. It also serves as the well of shared myth, history, and legendary associations that helps us comprehend the universe, both as individuals and as members of society.

If that's the case, you already have access to the myths and legends associated with each type of crystal. But if you want to access them even faster, you can also turn to the listings in this book.

The Magic of the Unseen World: Nature Spirits

One charming explanation for the power of crystals comes from the land of fable and myth, where invisible nature spirits known as *devas* manipulate events behind the scenes.

Devas are etheric, spiritual beings, and they are each associated with one of the four elements: earth, air, fire, or water. Earth elementals are also known as gnomes, and their numbers can include elves and brownies. Air elements are called sylphs, and they include fairies and cherubs. Fire elementals are salamanders, flaming creatures that usually look like lizards or balls of light. Water elementals are undines, such as nymphs, mermaids, and water spirits.

Every living thing—and some things we don't think of as "living," at least in the technical sense of the word—has its own deva. There are devas for trees, flowers, rivers, lakes, and springs. There are also devas for crystals, rocks, and stones.

Crystal devas represent the consciousness of crystals and the souls of stones. Together, they constitute the collective mind of the mineral kingdom. In this scenario, devas have the power to preserve, protect, and promote growth and well-being in the natural world, and they will happily work in partnership with like-minded humans.

As you start your work with crystals, you might want to imagine yourself communing with devas and the spirit of nature. Simply picture the spirit of a crystal in glowing, personified form, standing ready to help you in your efforts.

The Rainbow Connection

Crystals and Color

You can tell a lot about a crystal by its color and the magical way that a crystal interacts with light. In fact, color may be the single most important factor you will need to know in order to work with crystals.

Since the 1600s, when Isaac Newton used a prism to split sunlight into a rainbow of colors, scientists have recognized that light is a form of energy. That energy travels in waves, and the distance between each light wave is measured in terms of wavelength. Every wavelength has its own color—red, orange, yellow, green, blue, indigo, or violet.

In a way, color is an optical illusion. In the physical world, there are no colors—just light waves of different lengths. What's more, there are no colors in a darkened room. But where there is light, some objects absorb some wavelengths and reflect others. Red objects absorb every wavelength except red, which it reflects. Blue objects absorb every wavelength but blue. Yellow objects reflect only yellow light.

In other words, we don't really see color; we see light. The colors we perceive are simply reflections of light in the visible spectrum.

When you can see all the wavelengths of the visible light spectrum at once, you perceive white. Technically speaking, white isn't really a color at all; rather, white is the combination of all colors in the visible light spectrum. For that reason, visible light is sometimes called "white light." In the same way, black isn't a color, either. Technically speaking, black is simply the absence of any wavelength in the visible light spectrum.

For being colorless, however, black and white hold important symbolic significance, both in metaphysics as a whole, and in the more specialized field of crystallography. That's because all colors are imbued with traditional symbolism and significance.

Once you know those associations, you can go far in your work with crystals. In theory, you could even build an entire crystal collection based on nothing more than color and hue. (For a table of crystals by color, please see the Quick Reference Guides at the end of this book.)

White is the color of higher thought and higher consciousness. White symbolizes spiritual matters—pure, clean, and untainted by the dirt and debris of physical existence. White represents intuition and psychic ability. White also symbolizes innocence and purity. Use white crystals when you want to reflect on spiritual issues.

Black, on the other hand, symbolizes heavier issues. Obviously, black can be very grounding; the earth beneath our feet is dark and solid. But the color black can also represent grave forces like negativity and grief, and secret, dark emotions like anxiety and depression. Black is the color of mourning.

Black is also the color of night, when physical objects are obscured by darkness and our conscious thoughts succumb to the wild imaginings of our subconscious minds. You can use black crystals when you need to work with the darker forces of nature, like destruction and upheaval.

If anything can be seen at night, it's often by the reflected light of the moon or the glimmering of the stars. Normally, black absorbs every color in the spectrum of visible light. At the same time, however, a polished black surface is highly reflective. (Most scrying surfaces, used for gazing until psychic visions appear, are black.) Black is the color to use when you want to reflect on information that seems hidden, secret, dark or obscured, or when you want to reflect on your self, your situation, or the people around you. You can also use black crystals on a spiritual and symbolic level to reflect unwanted thoughts, emotions, energy, and behaviors back to their source.

Gray is a blend of black and white. A gray stone or crystal might remind you of a cooling shade, respite from a burning sun. On the other hand, a gray crystal might also represent the fog that can cloud your vision, smoke that obscures your sight, or the shadows that haunt your dreams. Use gray crystals when you want to cool down a situation, clear the fog of inconsistent thought and emotions, or explore your shadow issues.

Red is the color of passion. It's the color of blood coursing through your veins, sustaining your energy, and your essence. Red can represent anger or alarm—but it can also represent the fiery heat of love, the flames of desire, and sexuality, fertility, and creativity. Red can put you on alert—it can warn you of danger or compel you to stop in your tracks. Use red crystals when you feel especially passionate about an issue, or when you are dealing with matters of life and death.

Pink, a lighter, softer shade of red, represents more subdued passions. Shades of pink and rose are soothing, calming, even healing. They stir feelings of empathy, acceptance, friendship, and forgiveness. They may also inspire love and romance. Use pink crystals when you want to find peace, harmony, and tranquility.

Orange, a combination of red and yellow, combines passion and radiance, and reminds us of sunsets and warm tropical isles. Orange is the color of vitality and enjoyment—which means that orange crystals can help you feel energetic, vigorous, alert, and physically healthy.

Yellow, like the sun, is radiant and bright—so bright, in fact, that it is often associated with intellectual ability. Yellow crystals can make you think better, focus more intently, and concentrate on the task at hand. You can also use yellow crystals when you want to express your innate optimism, radiance, and brilliance.

Green is the color of nature, fertility, growth, renewal, and creativity—as well as the color of material abundance, prosperity, manifestation, and financial success. Green is both the color of the garden and the color of a U.S. dollar bill. Use a green stone if you want to grow plants—or grow your bank account.

Blue, the color of the sea and the sky, inspires tranquility. Blue is also associated with meditation, intuition, and psychic ability. Use blue crystals when you want to connect to the deep sea of consciousness, or when you want to soar to new heights for inspiration.

Indigo, the color of the midnight sky, symbolizes deep contemplation, wisdom, self-mastery, and spiritual realization. Use indigo crystals when you want to access cosmic wisdom.

Violet is the color of royalty. Violet once adorned emperors, kings, and queens, and the color represented their leadership and sovereignty over others. As a result, all purple shades connote luxury, wealth, and sophistication.

Brown is the color of the earth. It symbolizes grounding, stability, and the potentials inherent in fertile soil. Brown is also practical. Use brown stones and crystals when your goal is to be more grounded or when you would like to plant the seeds of new growth in your life.

Clear crystals, like transparent windows to the soul, remind us of the importance of clarity in both thought and vision. Use clear crystals when you want to think clearly or focus sharply on any issue. You can also visualize clear crystals filling with any color to use as substitutes for other colored crystals. Clear crystals can also amplify the energy and properties of other crystals.

Rainbow crystals—clear crystals that refract light like a prism—reflect every color of light in the visible spectrum. When you hold a rainbow crystal, you hold a sliver of the summer sky in your hand. Rainbow crystals remind us that we can reflect all the colors of the rainbow. They represent balance, harmony, and a bridge to other worlds. They also symbolize promise, hope, forgiveness, and cleansing, like a rainbow after a storm.

The Hand of God

Crystals in Their Natural Form

Crystals come in all shapes, from tumbled stones and cut crystals to natural formations like clusters, wands, and phantoms. While your mother may have told you not to judge people by their looks, you can certainly tell a lot about a crystal based on its appearance. In fact, a crystal's shape may determine its metaphysical function.

Abundance crystals are large crystals with an abundance of small crystals clustered around their base. You can use an abundance crystal when you want to multiply something that you have—like money. You can put a coin on an abundance crystal, for example, to indicate your desire for more change in your pocket. Because abundance crystals also feature one large crystal overlooking many small ones, they also symbolize parenthood, nurturing, and protection.

Artemis crystals, also known as candle crystals, are long, thin, clear quartz crystals with sharp, undamaged points. Like all wand-shaped crystals, Artemis crystals can help you direct your energy, focus your thoughts, and materialize your hopes and dreams. Artemis, the twin sister of Apollo, was the ancient Greek goddess of the hunt, and her crystals can be especially useful if you want to work on behalf of animals.

Barnacle crystals are covered, partially or completely, with delicate, smaller crystals—like barnacles clinging to the hull of a ship. Barnacle crystals are good for family, group, and community issues, especially if you are concerned about cooperation and trust.

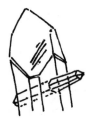

Bridge crystals, which are sometimes called penetrator crystals, are small crystals that run through a larger crystal. You can actually see a bridge crystal running through the body of the main crystal and sticking out on either side. Bridge crystals act like a bridge between worlds or a bridge between yourself and other people.

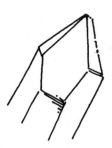

Cerridwen crystals have a large, five-sided facet at their tip or termination. They are named after the Celtic goddess Cerridwen, keeper of the cauldron of wisdom, inspiration, rebirth, and transformation. Like their namesake, Cerridwen crystals can be used for inspiration, intelligence, and knowledge, and invoked as a source of wisdom and counsel, or as a force for justice.

Channeling crystals are clear quartz crystals that typically have at least one large seven-sided face on one side of their tip and a triangular, three-sided face on the other. Some channeling crystals are also ordinary pieces of  clear quartz wrapped in copper wire. While channeling crystals make good tools for meditation, many people also believe that channeling crystals can help them channel wisdom and enlightenment from their spirit guides, guardian angels, unconscious minds, and higher selves. When you work with a channeling crystal, try to remain open to insights and inspirations that seem to come from nowhere.

Chips and pieces of larger crystals have the same properties as their parent stones. Crystal chips and pieces are the perfect size to include in medicine bags and mojo pouches. You can also display them in decorative vases or bowls, or string them together for jewelry.

Clusters are groups of crystals that have grown together on the same base, like miniature mountain ranges. Crystal clusters symbolize community—use them when you're dealing with issues of group cooperation, harmony, union, and friendship. They can also be used to cleanse other, smaller crystals—simply set the smaller crystals on top.

Curved crystals have a natural curve or bend, which can remind you of the importance of staying flexible.

Devic temple crystals are clear quartz crystals with rainbows of trapped air, water, and gas—commonly known as veils, foils, or fairy frost. Those rainbows, in conjunction with external and internal fractures in the crystal, tend to make the stones look like ancient temples, complete with stairways and doorways. Some people believe that devic temple crystals can facilitate communication with nature spirits like devas and elves.

Dolphin crystals are small crystals that seem to ride along the base of a larger stone. Dolphin crystals are playful, but they also represent communication with animals, unconditional love, loyalty, gentleness, and the importance of protecting and nurturing other living things.

Double-terminated crystals are naturally faceted on both ends because they grow in clay or gas bubbles, rather than on a base. The dual terminations allow energy to flow in both directions, which makes double-terminated crystals a good choice if you want to share you energy with another person. They also symbolize balance between two people, or between the body and the spirit, or between the conscious and the subconscious mind.

Dow crystals, also known as trans-channeling crystals, are named after JaneAnn Dow, a noted crystal healer and the author of *Crystal Journey*. The tip or termination of a Dow crystal has six faces— three of which are large faces with seven sides, while the other three are smaller faces with three sides each. Dow crystals work both for channeling and transmitting energy. They also are regarded as master crystals because they have the ability to both teach and heal.

Drusy crystals are clusters of small crystals that cover the surface of another mineral. Their tiny crystal points can encourage you to grow in new and unusual ways.

Elestial quartz crystals, also known as *crocodile quartz, jacare quartz,* and *skeletal quartz,* look like they have been built up, layer after layer, with etching-like markings all over their surfaces. The geometric patterns on their surface almost look like alligator skin. Some elestials have visible cavities, often layered or ribbed, sometimes pronounced enough to make the crystal seem hollow. Elestial crystals can also have many terminations; the points can look like a series of carved pyramids or a hand-drawn mountain range. Because they are so complex, elestials are good crystals to use if you have a lot of information to process.

Empathetic crystals are far from perfect—they have been chipped, cracked, broken, and damaged, sometimes extensively. Empathetic crystals have survived their own injuries, accidents, and trauma, however, so they represent empathy, compassion, and understanding. Like Chiron, the ancient centaur of Greek mythology, empathetic crystals are wounded healers.

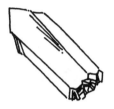

Extraterrestrial crystals have a single termination at one end and multiple terminations at the other, like a rocket ship with flames shooting from the bottom. Some people use them to connect with extraterrestrial beings.

Faden-lined crystals have a milky white thread of fluid or gas running through them, like a telephone line or an astral cord. The feathery, threadlike fibers usually run through the entire crystal, near the center. Faden-lined crystals are good for making connections and initiating new growth.

Family clusters are crystals that have one or two "parent" crystals surrounded by a number of smaller "children." Just as you would probably expect, family clusters represent family issues like protection and nurturing, as well as ancestry and heritage. Family clusters can be especially good to have around if you are a member of the "sandwich generation" and you find yourself caring for young children and aging parents at the same time.

Female crystals, with gentle, receptive "yin" energy, are usually cloudy or opaque, while male crystals, with active "yang" energy, are generally clear and transparent. Some crystals embody a balance of the two energies, while clusters can include very distinct mix of male and female crystals.

Gemini crystals, also called twin crys-  tals and soul mate crystals, have two points that share a single base. They not only share the same base, but there is no boundary between them. They have grown side by side for so long that their connection is seamless. Gemini crystals represent mergers, as well as partnerships and intimate relationships.

Generator crystals, also known as generating crystals, sending crystals, Merlin crystals, and energy guides, look like magic wands—or at least the magical crystal tip of a magic wand. They have six evenly spaced sides that come to a sharp and undamaged point on one end. Their symmetrical formation makes them a natural reminder of the wisdom, focus, and magical power of nature. Generator crystals can help you direct your energy so that you can manifest your ideas quickly and easily. You can use a generator crystal when you want to generate change in your life.

Geodes are hollow, round stones that are lined inside with crystals. Most geodes contain quartz, amethyst, citrine, or calcite. Study a geode when you want insight into your inner beauty or hidden talent, or when you want to visualize the makeup of the human soul.

Grounding crystals. While all crystals are grounding crystals to some extent, crystals with an eight-sided face are exceptionally grounding. They are somewhat rare, as most crystals have six sides. Grounding crystals can bring you back down to earth, literally and figuratively. Keep one near you to use as a reminder that you are a spiritual being in a physical body, and that you need to integrate both aspects.

Growth interference crystals seem to have been cut with a trim saw. In fact, they are quartz crystals that have had their growth interrupted by thin, flat, calcite crystals. Growth interference crystals are good for removing obstacles to our own growth, including the limits we impose on ourselves.

Hera crystals, also known as self-healed crystals, were broken at some point in their past, badly damaged, or severed or cut off from their original source. As time passed, however, they began to grow again, sealing and self-healing their broken ends with small triangular facets. Self-healed crystals signify renewal, rebirth, recuperation, and, of course, healing. Hera crystals are named in honor of the Greek goddess Hera, who dealt with her husband Zeus's infidelities by becoming a strong, self-sufficient woman.

Holed stones are stones that literally have holes worn through them by weather, water, or even by small living creatures. While sacred to the Norse god Odin, holed stones are also connected to goddess lore and associated with feminine wisdom, fertility, motherhood, and protection. According to legend, if you look through a holed stone by the light of a full moon, you can see into the spirit world. Holed stones can also help people who suffer from nightmares.

Included crystals have inclusions—particles of foreign matter, such as dirt, dust, other minerals, or pockets of water or oil.

Inner child crystals are actually two crystals in one—they consist of one small crystal partly embedded within a larger stone. The smaller crystal usually extends a bit from the larger crystal, as well. Inner child crystals symbolize buried memories and emotions, and they are especially recommended for people who have had painful or traumatic childhoods.

Isis crystals are a lot like Cerridwen crystals. They have a five-sided facet at their tip. The bottom edges of the pentagon, which point up and out, represent reaching out into the world; the top lines come back together, symbolizing spiritual focus. Isis crystals are named in honor of the Egyptian goddess Isis, who worked tirelessly to reassemble and revive her husband Osiris after he was murdered and dismembered. Isis crystals are especially useful if you must deal with issues of fidelity or grief. After Osiris's death, Isis magically conceived his child, so Isis crystals represent fertility, creativity, and motherhood as well. Isis crystals aren't just for women; if you're a man who wonders what women want, pick up an Isis. An Isis crystal will help you deal with your girlfriend or wife, and help you understand your mother, sisters, daughters, and female co-workers, too.

Japanese law twins are conjoined at the bottom, so they form a "V" or a heart shape. Japanese law twins symbolize synthesis.

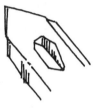

Key crystals have a three-sided or six-sided indented shape that narrows as it goes into the crystal—like a keyhole. You can use a key crystal if you would like to unlock secrets, uncover hidden information, or understand illusive concepts.

Laser wand crystals are long and slender. They're a little bit wider at the base than at the tip, and they taper gradually toward one end. Like magic wands, laser wand crystals are good for clearing negativity, creating protective barriers, and focusing energy—especially healing energy.

Left-handed crystals have an extra facet somewhere on the left side of their largest face or termination. Left-handed crystals can help you become more creative, insightful, intuitive, and psychic.

Lifepath crystals are long and thin, with one side that's completely smooth. Use a lifepath crystal if you want to forge a smoother path in your life.

Male crystals, with active "yang" energy, are generally clear and transparent, while female crystals, with gentle, receptive "yin" energy, are usually cloudy or opaque. Some crystals embody a balance of the two energies, while clusters can include very distinct mix of male and female crystals.

Manifestation crystals feature a small crystal totally encased within a larger crystal. Manifestation crystals can help you manifest the hopes, plans, and dreams that lie buried inside you. Manifestation crystals can also represent buried memories and emotions, and they can be used like inner child crystals for people who have had painful or traumatic childhoods.

Mythic crystals are milky quartz crystals with terminations on both ends. Mythic crystals seem like solidified clouds, and it's not hard to imagine that when you gaze into a mythic crystal, you are actually gazing into the swirling mists of time. Some people have even suggested that mythic crystals could hold the secrets of ancient myths and archetypes. Mythic crystals are especially good to use during meditation.

Needle crystals are very long and very narrow, which makes them well suited for focusing energy or for sewing the pieces of your soul back together.

Parity crystals come in clusters of evenly sized stones. Parity means equality, and parity crystals are reminders that all people are equal.

Phantom crystals. At some point in their growth cycle, phantom crystals stopped growing, but then started up again. The evidence of their halted development lingers on: you can see the faint outline of their former selves still trapped inside. Sometimes, that ghostly shadow is a result of foreign materials or impurities that settled on the crystal as it grew. When you look at a phantom crystal, you might see the ghostly specter of one of your past lives, or the remains of a long-lost relationship that has left a fading imprint on your soul. Phantom crystals could even remind you of the various roles you have played in your life, or of the evolution you've undergone through time and place. Phantom crystals can also suggest that it may be time for you to resume your growth after a period of rest and reflection.

Pixilated crystals, also called enchanted crystals, are double-terminated clear quartz crystals filled with rainbows and fairy frost. Like the misty landmarks of a dream, pixilated crystals awaken us to the existence of mythical beings like pixies, elves, gnomes, and fairies, as well as plant and animal devas.

Quantum crystals consist of three or more double-terminated crystals joined together. *Quantum* is Latin for "amount," and the term generally refers to a very small measure or quantity. The statistical odds against finding a quantum crystal make them especially suited to use as agents of transition and transformation. If you have a quantum crystal, use it to help you bring about major changes in your life.

Quartz points are bits and pieces of quartz crystal tips and terminations. Quartz points are especially good for transmitting information throughout a grid or layout—like those used in healing. Quartz points will naturally focus and intensify energy in any direction they are aimed. Some people believe that terminations can even work like knives to cut through blocked energy. Quartz points are beautiful when grouped together, and they can unify a pattern of crystals laid out for meditation or healing work.

Rainbow crystals are a physical manifestation of pure white light. They're not uncommon—many clear quartz crystals work like prisms, and refract the visible light spectrum through embedded cracks, fractures, veils, or trapped air and water. Rainbow crystals symbolize boundless possibilities, as well as joy, hope, optimism, forgiveness, and fresh new beginnings. Rainbow crystals make especially nice gifts.

Receiving crystals have one broad, flat face. Sometimes, crystal healers hold the flat face against a sick or injured part of the body to draw out the negative energy, or they place them alongside the heart or the head to draw out negative thoughts and feelings. You could also try holding a receiving crystal in your left hand (which is your receptive hand, if you are right-handed) and a projecting crystal in your right hand to give and receive energy at the same time.

Record-keeper crystals have small, triangular markings on their surface. Some of those markings are raised, while others seem to be engraved into the surface. The marks can be

hard to see, so you may need to hold your crystal in bright light to find them. Each mark is associated with a single, specific lesson for the person who holds it. According to those who work with record keepers, sometimes the triangular markings seem to appear and disappear.

The lore associated with record keeper crystals may seem fantastic. Some people believe that record keeper crystals were programmed by ancient civilizations to hold vital information for future generations, and then buried deep in the earth. Some people also believe that record keeper crystals can materialize out of thin air. Record keeper crystals can be helpful to those who seek ancient secrets, esoteric wisdom, or information about their past lives.

Right-handed crystals have an extra facet somewhere on the right side of their largest face or termination. Right-handed crystals can help you become more rational, logical, and analytical. When you work with right-handed crystals, hold them in your right hand.

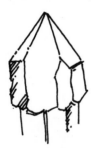

Scepter crystals look very much like the scepters held by kings and queens, which were symbols of their worldly power. They result when a normal, wand-shaped crystal begins a second stage of growth, which looks like the tip of a scepter— heavier and wider than the stem. You can use a scepter crystal when you want to wield power over your life and your environment.

Because scepter crystals are also very phallic in shape, you can use them when you want to draw upon masculine energy and force, or when you want to scatter the seeds of new ideas and generate new projects.

Selene crystals are named in honor of Selene, the eternally beautiful Greek goddess of the moon. Selene crystals have rounded, moon-shaped inclusions, such as bubbles of air, water, and oil. Selene crystals will remind you of the richness and fullness of the moon, as well as the regular cycles of the lunar orb. Use a Selene crystal if you are dealing with issues that seem to come and go on a regular basis. Because Selene was also said to be the mother of fifty children, you can also use Selene crystals if you are pregnant, trying to get pregnant, raising children, or dealing with your own mother.

Seven-sided crystals have seven sides and seven natural terminations at the tip. Because seven is an especially mystical number associated with the seven heavens, the seven chakras, the seven days of the week, and more, a seven-faceted crystal enhances introspection, serenity, mysticism, spiritual attainment, transcendence, and peace.

Shovel crystals have one facet shaped like a shovel, which makes them especially well suited for use when you need to dig for information.

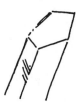

Singing crystals are small, thin, cylindrical crystals that make a high-pitched singing or tinkling sound when rubbed or rolled together. Their music can be used to clear the air, get energy flowing, and inspire creativity.

Six-sided crystals are very common; most quartz crystals have six sides. Single-terminated crystals are flat on the bottom (because they grow from a rocky base), and they usually come to a single point at the tip or termination. Terminations naturally focus, intensify, and direct energy in any direction they are aimed. Some people believe that terminations can even work like knives to cut through blocked energy.

Six-sided crystals may be common, but their symbolism is still quite moving. The six sides of a hexagon are said to correspond to the six chakras, or energy centers in the human body. The point on the tip or termination of a six-sided crystal corresponds to the seventh chakra, just above the head.

 **Spiral crystals** have a spiral shape and a clearly visible, twisted pattern of growth. They may remind you of light and sound waves winding their way through space, or a spiral staircase rising to higher planes of consciousness. Spiral crystals also seem to embody the spiraling double helix of human DNA. You can use a spiral crystal if you want to access your higher self, or if you want to work with the gifts and talents you inherited from your parents and grandparents. Because spiral crystals could also re-

mind you of the wavelike patterns of light and sound, you can also use one if you want to develop your communication skills.

Tabular crystals, sometimes called tabby crystals, are flat and rectangular, like a stone tablet or a table. Generally speaking, two sides of a tabular crystal are at least twice as wide as the other two sides. Tabular crystals symbolize the kind of communication that can take place across a table. They are good for planning work with other people, as well as face-to-face discussion, dialogue, and dispute resolution.

Timeline crystals have one rectangular face or facet, like a parallelogram, that leans to the right or the left. When we construct a written time-line, we tend to put events of the past on the left, events of the present in the center, and future occurrences on the right. For that reason, crystals 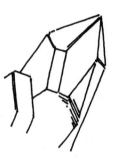 with a facet that leans to the left are good for accessing information from the past, and crystals with a facet that leans to the right are good for accessing information from the future.

Transmitter crystals have two symmetrical seven-sided faces with a perfect triangular face between them.

Trigger crystals have a little crystal growing from their sides, like the trigger on a gun. To activate a trigger crystal for meditation, reflection, or divination, gently squeeze the trigger.

Wands are slender, clear quartz crystals. When you hold a wand in your hand, it automatically extends your own power by metaphorically extending your reach. Wands can help make your wishes, dreams, and prayers come true.

Wands are powerful crystals. Never point a wand at anyone in jest, and never wish for anything negative when working with a wand.

Window crystals have an extra diamond-shaped face on the termination, large enough to be considered a seventh facet. (Most crystals have six faces on their terminations.) Just as you might expect, those windows represent windows into the soul or the spirit world.

Yin-yang crystals are milky, cloudy, or opaque on one end, which represents their gentle, receptive "yin" energy. On the other end, they are clear and transparent, in line with active "yang" energy. Use a yin-yang crystal when you need to find a balance between any two extremes.

Shaping Up

Carved and Polished Crystals

Crystals come in a wide range of shapes and sizes—some natural and some augmented with a little help from modern technology.

Amulets are tokens and charms that are typically carved out of stone. They can be worn or carried for good luck, but they are usually carried for protection from evil.

Cabochons are gemstones that have been cut and polished into smooth domes. The word cabochon comes from the French word *caboche*, which means "head." Cabochons don't have facets.

Eggs symbolize fertility, for obvious reasons, as well as related concepts like potential, new development, and the early stages of creation. Eggs also represent safety and protection from outside elements. Egg-shaped crystals and stones can sometimes symbolize the *cosmic egg*, the mythical source of all creation.

Hearts represent romantic love and emotional healing.

Massage wands are smooth, palm-size wands or rods. Massage wands fit nicely in the hand, and they can be a great aid in massage and healing. Massage wands are usually rounded at one end, to glide smoothly over the body, and pointed at the other for acupressure, reflexology, or chakra healing. You can roll a massage wand over clothes, or use one with oil on bare skin.

Obelisks are four-sided pillars that terminate in a pyramid shape. Many classic monuments, like the Washington Monument, are obelisks. Symbolically, an obelisk can discharge tension and high-pressure energy through its tip, sending it high into the atmosphere to be dissipated and dispersed. An obelisk can also draw energy in from the upper atmosphere and ground that energy through its base.

Pyramids, like the famous landmarks in Egypt and Central America, have a square base and four triangle-shaped sides. A pyramid can draw spiritual energy through its apex and ground it solidly at its base. Pyramids represent a blend of the spiritual and physical. They are long lasting and stable, and they serve as a valuable reminder of ancient architecture, ancient beliefs, and the power of sacred geometry. Pyramid crystals can be used to focus and ground energy, and some people also use pyramids of metal and glass to charge their crystals.

Skulls, eerie carved crystals in the shape of miniature human heads, have been credited with amazing supernatural powers. The most famous crystal skull was said to be discovered in 1924 by F. A. Mitchell-Hedges, a British adventurer, whose teenage daughter found the skull under an ancient altar in some ancient Mayan ruins. The skull is life-sized, and it looks like a real human skull—right down to the movable jawbone. It weighs more than eleven pounds, all carved from a single piece of quartz. Oddly enough, the skull appears to have been carved against the natural axis of the stone, which should have shattered the crystal. There are no tool marks or scratches on the crystal, either, which means that researchers can't explain how it was produced.

Some people believe that crystal skulls were used in ancient religious ceremonies, in which priests would manipulate the skulls and make them seem to speak to their congregants. Some people believe crystal skulls contain ancient secrets and long-lost wisdom. Some people also believe that crystal skulls are healing oracles, with the power to shepherd humanity into a new age of peace and harmony.

Miniature crystal skulls, carved from a wide variety of quartz, are widely available. You can use a crystal skull to tap into your own source of ancient wisdom and connect to humanity on a wide scale.

Spheres and crystal balls—which are, after all, three-dimensional circles—symbolize the cyclical nature of life and the spherical construction of the universe. They remind us of unity and completion, and events coming full circle. They remind us of the earth itself, a giant, spinning globe. They remind us of potency and possibility, like the rounded form of a pregnant woman. Circles symbolize infinity because they have no beginning and no end. They also represent harmony because there are no sharp angles or edges.

Talismans are ornate, carved objects, often made of engraved metal and ornamented with carved crystals and stones. Talismans are worn for luck; they are designed to bring good things to their wearers.

Totems are crystals that have been carved in the shape of an animal or a mythical creature. Totems can symbolize your spirit, your cultural traditions, or your membership in a tribe or a community. Totems can come in any shape, but some popular choices include bears, which symbolize ferocious maternal instincts and protection; cats, which symbolize independence, regal bearing, agility, multiple lives, and magic; dragons, which symbolize a fiery spirit, guardianship, and power over obstacles and foes; owls, which symbolize wisdom and night vision; rabbits, which symbolize fertility and luck; snakes, which symbolize rebirth, sexuality, wisdom, and temptation; turtles, which symbolize longevity, self-defense, and self-sufficiency; and wolves, which symbolize one's primal nature and untamed spirit.

Tumbled stones. At the seashore, Mother Nature washes rocks and pebbles in sand and salt water until they are polished, beautiful, and smooth. Rock tumblers do the same thing by tossing and mixing stones and crystals for days or weeks on end in a gritty polishing mix.

Tumbled stones are beautiful. They're usually so polished they look wet; that polish also serves to liberate the color and shine that can be buried in a crystal's rough exterior.

Tumbled stones are durable. By the time they have made it through a month in a rock tumbler, they won't scratch each other or break when they come into contact with each other, like uncut and unpolished crystals might.

Tumbled stones are affordable. You can buy them by the piece, by the bag, or by the pound.

It's easy to identify stones and crystals that have been tumbled: their true colors are more vivid, and their characteristics are more recognizable. It's easy to store and display tumbled stones, too. You can keep them together in a single dish or a drawstring bag—they need far less special treatment than crystals and stones in their natural state. That makes tumbled stones highly portable, too. They fit smoothly in a pocket or a purse, which also makes it easy to give them away as impromptu gifts and good luck charms.

Tumbled stones seem ready-made for laying on in healing sessions or gridwork. They don't have any rough edges that could poke or scratch, and they are so smooth that they will usually simply fall off or roll away when their work is done.

Vogel-cut crystals were the brainchild of Marcel Vogel, an IBM scientist who decided to cut quartz into the shape of the Kabbalistic tree of life, a symbolic diagram that illustrates the structure of the universe. Both ends of a Vogel-cut crystal are terminated, but one end is larger and cut at a

51-degree angle. Vogel-cut crystals are beautiful, and those who own them say they can amplify and focus energy better than uncut crystals or crystals that have been cut into other shapes.

Worry stones are flat, with a shallow groove carved into one side. Just as the name implies, when you are anxious or worried, you can hold a worry stone in the palm of your hand and rub it back and forth with your thumb to calm down.

Pleased to Meet You

Getting to Know Your Crystals

How do you learn what an individual crystal can do? How can you discover its specific strengths, its properties, and its gifts?

Go right to the source: the crystal. The easiest, most efficient way to know your crystals is to spend time with them.

Hold your crystals. When you add a new crystal to your collection, simply hold it and ask, "What do you have to teach me?" Yes, it's a little hooky spooky—but you might be pleasantly surprised by the answers you receive. You might hear a word, a phrase, or a sentence in your head. You might hear a snippet of song. You might get a visual impression, or sense an emotion, or simply discover that your new crystal wants you to hone your intuitive skills a little more.

Carry your crystals. Whether you're heading off on a world cruise or a trip to the corner market, take a few crystals with you in your pocket or your purse.

Get your mojo workin'. You can tuck small crystals into a medicine pouch or mojo bag. Medicine bags are sacred to some Native American cultures, who typically made them of animal skins. Mojo bags are a development of the Deep South, where hoodoo practitioners usually crafted them of flannel or felt.

You can make either type of bag quickly and easily. Simply buy a ready-made bag, or use the fabric or material of your choice and sew a small drawstring pouch. Fill it with magical crystals, herbs, amulets, and talismans. Tie your medicine or mojo bag to a string and wear it around your neck, tucked underneath your shirt.

Most people keep their medicine and mojo bags private and open them only when they need to access their contents for spiritual work.

Wear your crystals. You may already own some gemstone jewelry. Whether polished, cut, or carved, genuine gemstones have the same mystic properties as crystals in their natural state. You can also buy crystals that have been drilled so that you can hang them on a chain or a velvet cord, crystal beads for stringing, or wire wraps and cages so you can wear your crystals as jewelry.

Keep your crystals in sight. Keep crystals on your desk, your nightstand, by your phone, or on your kitchen table. With just a little extra effort, you can even create crystal displays that will add depth and drama to your collection.

Set the stage. As you start to surround yourself with crystals, you will probably want to put them in obvious places, such as bookshelves, coffee tables, and fireplace mantles. While windowsills are a good display area for some stones, be careful about which crystals you leave in the sun. Many crystals will fade, change color, or lose their color completely if they are exposed to direct sunlight. Choose a shady spot for your amethyst, apatite, aquamarine, aventurine, beryl, celestite, citrine, fluorite, kunzite, rose quartz, sapphire, and smoky quartz.

Whatever you do, don't treat your crystals like an ordinary rock collection. Avoid tucking your stones into little boxes with tissue paper liners and reference tags—unless, of course, you plan to have a very large collection, in which case you could put a tiny removable sticker with a numbered key on the bottom of each one, corresponding to notes and records in your crystals journal. But do try to avoid the temptation to close your crystals up in drawers and cabinets. Crystals can't work their magic if they're in storage. The whole point of having crystals is to enjoy them, even when you're not actually holding them.

While you could put some of your crystals in glass-front display cases, you will get the most out of your crystals if you place them strategically throughout your home, where air can circulate freely around them. The crystals can sparkle in sun and moonlight, and their presence can lift and energize everybody's mood.

Try the following techniques:

- For a decorator impact, group your crystals by color. From an aesthetic perspective, odd-numbered groupings look best. Try arranging your crystals in groups of three, five, or seven.

- Unify your displays by putting your crystals on trays, mirrored tiles, or pedestals.

- Arrange your crystals on loosely gathered scarves or swatches of fabric.

- Try grouping your crystals around a tabletop fountain.

- Stack your metaphysical books on their sides, like shelves, and display your crystals on top of the books.

- Make tiered risers by draping fabric over boxes or blocks of wood.

- Categorize your collection by shape, particularly if you recognize the metaphysical properties of each formation.

- Keep crystal balls and egg-shaped crystals from rolling around by setting them on hematite rings.

- Display any type or shape of crystal on plastic, wood, and metal stands.

- Keep tumbled stones in baskets, bowls, and clear glass jars.

- Tuck flowers and greenery around your crystals to make your crystals look like part of an outdoor landscape.

- Intersperse your display with other natural elements, such as feathers, driftwood, and shells.

- Display your crystals alongside figurines and small statues, or framed photographs of people you love.

- Tuck prayer cards or affirmations underneath some of your crystals.

- Add candles and incense burners to your collection.

- As seasons change, rearrange your displays. Try to incorporate elements that reflect the outside world, such as buds and blossoms in spring, cut flowers in summer, colored leaves in fall, and pine branches and pinecones in the winter.

- Create an altar to remind yourself of the beauty and sacredness of the physical objects in your life—not only the crystals, but also tokens and reminders of the people and activities you love. Your altar could be the top of a bedroom dresser, the mantle in your living room, a shelf in the kitchen, or a table in your front hall—anywhere you have the space and the desire to display your most meaningful items.

- Develop a calming Zen meditation garden by strategically placing your crystals in a shallow box or a tray filled with sand. Use a miniature rake, a stick, or your fingertips to sculpt waves and swirling patterns in the sand around the crystals.

Keep your crystals out and on display, and their beauty and charm will fill your home—and your heart—with light and energy.

Treat Me Right

The Care and Feeding of Crystals

Once you find your crystals and bring them home, you'll need to prepare them for your use. Here are some simple starting techniques.

How to Clean Your Crystals

When you first get a crystal, you may want to cleanse it, both physically and spiritually. It might be dirty, or it might have picked up some unwanted vibrations from people who have handled it. You should also clean any crystals you have used in healing to ensure that they don't retain any vestiges of disease or poor health.

If your crystals seem physically dirty, dusty, or grimy, cleaning them is easy—wipe them with a damp washcloth or a soft dust rag. If they are especially grubby, you can usually wash them with water and a gentle dishwashing detergent. Be careful not to subject your crystals to extreme temperature changes, of course; if you plunge a cold crystal into a sink full of hot water, it could crack.

But some crystals need more than just a quick wipe with a wet rag—they need a metaphysical spit and polish, too. In other words, you may need to take cleaning one step further and give your crystals a good clearing.

How to Clear Your Crystals

Because crystals can store energy, they can hold on to more than just fingerprints. They can retain psychic energy, too, from anyone who handles them.

Most crystal aficionados agree that you should cleanse and clear new crystals whenever you acquire them. Some also suggest that you should clear them whenever other people touch them. In fact, some even go so far as to suggest that you shouldn't allow others to handle your crystals. Your stones, they suggest, are only your own. If you let other people work with them, your crystals will lose their focus, their energy will be dissipated, and they'll have less power to affect and change your life.

That argument works both ways, though. If your friends, family members, and loved ones pick up your crystals, they could actually imbue them with positive emotions. In fact, people who look at crystals usually pick them up to admire them, which could only have a positive affect on your collection.

What's more, there is probably enough power inside a crystal to go around. After all, every crystal ever mined has been around for far longer than most of us can imagine . . . and those crystals will probably still be here long after we're gone. Their energy can't be dissipated or destroyed simply by being handled for a few moments.

Granted, if someone who is feeling sad, angry, depressed, or frustrated picks up your crystals, you might want to polish them up a bit and return them to a state of positive balance. And if you use your crystals for healing or for reflection on dark and shadowy issues, you'll definitely want to clear them afterward.

Here are some common crystal-clearing techniques you can try:

Breath. The easiest way to clear a crystal is simply to hold it with both hands, and gently blow a slow, steady stream of air over and around the stone. How long you blow doesn't matter. How hard you blow doesn't matter. The only thing that truly makes a difference is that you intend to clear your crystal, and that you focus all of your energy and attention to that task, even just for a moment.

White light visualization. You can also accomplish a remarkably effective cleansing and clearing through visualization. First, sit very still—preferably on the ground, but if you'd rather, sit in a chair with your feet firmly planted on the floor. Take several deep breaths. Clear your mind, concentrating only on your breathing. With each breath, imagine that the space around you is growing lighter and lighter. Then envision waves of white light surrounding your crystals, shimmering, glowing, and filling them with clear, clean energy.

A bit of polish. Wipe your crystals clean with a soft cloth, imagining that you are also wiping them clean of stored impressions, emotions, programming, or patterning.

A pinch of salt. Salt is a traditional method of cleaning and clearing crystals. Some people suggest that you soak your stones in salt water or immerse them in a bowl of coarse salt. Sea salt is especially recommended, because it's natural—but any type of salt will do. Salt is a crystal itself, and it has long been associated with purification.

Unfortunately, salt can work its way into the tiny cracks and fissures of a crystal, even those that are practically invisible to the naked eye. That could damage the crystal.

If you want to soak your crystals in salt water, make sure they are solid, without any fractures or breaks that could make them vulnerable to further damage. If you want to immerse your crystals in a container of salt, consider wrapping it in cloth, first. If you want to play it completely safe, try sprinkling just a few grains of salt over or around your crystals, for the same end result.

Smudging. For centuries, people in almost every culture have burned herbs for emotional and spiritual purification. In Western cultures, for example, incense is believed to carry one's prayers to heaven.

The Native American practice of smudging is one that seems to work especially well with crystals. You'll need a smudge stick, which you can make yourself or find in a specialty shop. Smudge sticks are simply bundles of dried cedar, sage, and lavender, wrapped with string. They look a little like big, fat cigars.

You'll also need a fireproof dish to hold the smudge stick. Most people use a ceramic dish, like an ashtray, or a large seashell filled with sand, which symbolizes the element of water and provides a counterbalance to the fire and smoke of the smudge stick.

Light one end of the smudge stick with a match. Gently blow out the flame, but don't blow so hard you extinguish the smudge stick completely. You want the tip to glow red, like incense, so that it continues to smolder and smoke.

You can hold your crystals in the smoke of a smudge stick, or use a feather to gently fan the smoke over and around them.

Candle magic. You can also clear your crystals by passing them through the light, heat, and smoke of a candle. You don't need to pass them directly through the flame—no one wants you or your crystals to undergo any sort of trial by fire. Candle clearing is a good alternative to smudging, especially if you don't like the smell of most smudge sticks.

Try to use a candle that hasn't been used for any other purpose. Your crystals won't get clean if your cleansing agent is itself imbued with leftover birthday wishes, snippets of dinnertime conversation, or any reminder of its last duty station on your bedroom dresser.

For general cleansing, white candles work best because they symbolize purity and new beginnings. If you have a specific purpose in mind for the crystal you're clearing, however, you might want to experiment with using a color that symbolizes your intention: red for love and passion, for example, or blue for tranquility. You might also want to match your candles to the colors of your crystals to refill them with energy that corresponds to their metaphysical properties.

Babbling brook. If you have access to the fresh running water of a river or a stream, or the constant movement of an ocean or a sea, take your crystals there and give them a rinse. As you hold your crystals under the water, imagine that the waves and currents are washing away any old programming or negativity within the stones. If you are pressed for time, you can accomplish the same thing by holding your crystals under running water at the kitchen sink. In that case, imagine yourself in a natural setting—the experience will calm your spirit and remind you that crystals are a gift from nature.

Standing water. You could even leave your crystals next to a dish of water for a day or two. Set the water out with the express intention that it will attract and absorb any negativity stuck in the crystals. Once you're done, don't give the water to pets or plants. It might still look clean, but it will be metaphorically filthy. Pour it down the drain.

Wind power. Hold your crystals in a gentle breeze, and imagine the wind blowing away any backlog of negativity.

Raindrops. A good soaking rain might be the perfect way to refresh your crystal collection. Just set your crystals outside when the skies start to cloud up, and let the raindrops dance across their surface. When the storm passes, give your crystals a quick polish with a clean dry towel, and they will be springtime fresh and clean.

Sound. Ring out the old and ring in the new by using sound waves to clear your crystals. Sound can clear a room just as effectively as light. It has the added benefit of reenergizing a space. Sound can literally work to harmonize both you and your crystals. You can play music, ring a bell, strike a gong, or try your hand at a Buddhist singing bowl.

Blessing. You may want to develop a blessing to clean and clear your crystals. Your blessing can be short and sweet, like this: "May you be filled with light and love, and open to whatever comes." Or you could use this blessing:

Crystals red and crystals blue,
Crystals green and yellow, too
As you share your light and love,
May you share blessings from above.

David Spangler is the author of *Blessing: The Art and the Practice*, in which he described how he was once called upon to bless a stone.

As I held it in my hand, I took myself into my blessing place and began to love this stone. I admired it, I attuned to its hardness, its earthiness, working my way down into it through my love for it. As I did, the spirit of the stone began to open and I found myself in touch with what I could only describe as the spirit of the earth or at least of its mineral nature. It seemed I could trace a line of connection from that stone right to the earth's molten core. At the same time, another line of connection ran out into space, into the ubiquitousness of stone throughout the universe. In short, this little stone had become a portal for me into a vast community of spiritual beings who embodied the qualities of the mineral kingdom and its molecular and atomic structures throughout creation.

Holding this stone in my hand, it felt just like a small living creature, particularly as I felt the energy coming from this larger community of "mineral beings," and I proceeded to bless it just as I would any other living being. I attuned as best I could to the larger community from which it seemed to come, inviting its combined energy into the process, using myself as a vessel with which to receive and focus the blessing.[1]

Prayer. While closely related to blessing, a prayer may be the perfect way to clear your crystals. You can devise a prayer of your own, or rely on a traditional prayer like "Come, Holy Spirit."

Come, Holy Spirit.
Fill the hearts of your faithful and make the fire
of your love burn within them.
Send forth your spirit and there shall be
another creation.
And you shall renew the face of the earth.

Chanting. You might want to clear your crystals by chanting a Buddhist mantra, such as *"Om lokah samastha sukhino bhavantu,"* which means "May this world be established

---

1. David Spangler, *Blessing: The Art and the Practice* (New York: Riverhead Books, 2001), 298–299.

with a sense of well-being and happiness," or *"Om mani pedme hum,"* which inspires compassion.

Go green. Just as living, growing plants can help purify the air in your house, they can also help detoxify your used crystals. Simply place your crystals around the base of your houseplants—or nestle them against the flowers in your garden—and let the spirit of nature step in to spiff them up.

Crystal cluster. Most crystals grow in communities, so they are used to being together. And just as people often gather for strength and support, many crystal experts report that their stones seem to lighten and brighten when they are kept in close quarters. If you have a small crystal that needs recharging, put it on top of an amethyst cluster or larger quartz crystal for a few days.

Plants and crystal clusters have the added advantage of being a source of new energy for your stones.

Four elements. For an especially powerful cleansing and charging session, incorporate a representation of all four elements in your work: earth, air, fire, and water. Combine a sprinkling of salt, for earth; the smoke of a smudge stick or the scented perfume of incense, for air; the light of a burning candle, for fire; and a sprinkling of pure spring water.

How to Charge Your Crystals

Once you use your crystals for any length of time, you may find that they feel drained of some of their power and force, just as if you had drained their batteries.

Not to worry: just plug them back in to another source of energy and let them recharge.

Solar flair. The most obvious source of energy, for crystals or for any of us on earth, is the sun. Many crystal experts swear that a few hours of sunshine will clear away any clouds in your crystals' cosmic complexion and refill them with pure, bright light. You must use caution, however, or you could get burned—literally. Sunlight can pass through a crystal like a magnifying glass and start a fire, so make sure you're not focusing the sun's rays on your favorite tablecloth or a stack of old newspapers.

Also, remember that sunlight can damage some crystals. A number of stones will fade, change color, or lose their color completely if they are exposed to direct sunlight, including amethyst, apatite, aquamarine, aventurine, beryl, celestite, citrine, fluorite, kunzite, rose quartz, sapphire, and smoky quartz.

Moonlighting. You can also enhance the glow of your crystals by bathing them in the light of the silvery moon. The light of a waxing or full moon, which symbolizes growth and fulfillment, is generally better for recharging than a waning moon, in which the orb's strength and power is on the decrease.

Buried treasure. If your crystals seem worn out and tired, let them go home to mother for a few days. Simply take them back to their source and bury them—temporarily— safely in the arms of Mother Earth. If you don't want your crystals to get dirty, wrap them in fabric or slip them into a paper bag before you bury them. Be sure to mark their location, too, so you can find them when it's time for them to be reborn.

Close companions. As plants and flowers grow, they energize the atmosphere around them. Tuck your crystals inside your pots and planters, and let them soak up the companionable energy of your healthy indoor greenery.

How to Program Your Crystals

If you plan to do any metaphysical work with your crystals, you should program them with a fail-safe device—a guarantee, of sorts, that their power can only be used for good. While your intentions may always be pure, it's not possible to recognize all of the ramifications of every action, especially when other people are involved.

When you get a new crystal, simply cleanse it, clear it, and hold it in your hands. Then say the following verse, or improvise something similar, in your own words:

Whether you help many,
Or whether you help one,
Your power will be used for good;
The process will harm none.

On a more practical level, you can also program your crystals to help you reach specific goals. Whether you want to feel healthier, be more physically active, or find more satisfaction in your relationships, you can program a crystal to remind you of the life you want to lead—and help you bring that life into being.

You will have the most success if you program your crystals in positive terms, rather than negative. Try not to think in terms of things you want to eliminate from your life; instead, focus on the ideals and goals you want to achieve. If you want to lose weight, for example, don't program a crystal to help you eat less. Program one, instead, to help you exercise more and eat more sensibly. If you want to give up smoking, program a crystal to help you relax and spend more time in meditation, where you can experience the pleasure of simple, deep breathing. If you want to stop arguing with someone you love, program a crystal to help you find activities you can share and enjoy with friends and family members.

You can program a crystal to serve as a tangible reminder of a wish, a goal, or an intention. Programming a crystal is a lot easier than programming a computer, too. Here is a simple, step-by-step guide.

- First, make sure that the crystal you're working with has been cleansed and cleared of any old programming that could interfere with the new schedule you have in mind.

- Hold the crystal in your hand.

- Visualize your goal or intention, clearly and in as much detail as you can muster. Picture exactly how your intention will look and feel. Imagine the sensations you will experience when it comes to fruition: sights, sounds, tastes, smells.

- As you visualize your intention, imagine it flowing from your mind into the crystal, deeper and deeper with each breath you exhale.

- At the same time, verbalize your intention. Put it in terms of an affirmation, and say it aloud. If you are programming your crystal for prosperity, for example, say, "Wealth, prosperity, and abundance are mine."

- If you prefer, you can write your intention on a piece of paper and tuck it underneath your crystal overnight.

- Carry the crystal with you, and whenever you are tempted to head for the office vending machines, touch the crystal for a reminder of your new, healthier lifestyle.

- A programmed crystal also makes a lovely gift. You can tell the recipient that you chose the crystal for them to carry as a good luck charm, or for any purpose you have in mind.

Barriers and Shields

You might have heard that crystals can be used for protection. It's true: you can use dark-colored stones like hematite, magnetite, and smoky quartz to absorb negative energy. You can use light-colored stones like moonstone, selenite, and quartz to deflect harmful thoughts and reflect dangerous intentions back to their source. You can even sprinkle ordinary salt crystals around perimeters and entryways to keep unwanted visitors out or bar destructive forces from entering your space.

But before you start throwing up stone walls and raising a crystal drawbridge, you might want to consider a more positive approach.

Granted, it's natural to think in terms of what you don't want in your life. When you feel tired, used, and run down, sometimes all you can imagine is simply eliminating the factors that are wearing you out. If you feel threatened—either physically, spiritually, emotionally, or mentally—you need to rally whatever support you can muster for your defense. You may need to program your crystals as guardians and shields, if it will make you feel more secure.

On the other hand, you might also want to consider programming your crystals in terms of feeling positive, optimistic, and loved. The affirmation "I am safe here" is simply more encouraging and affirming than "I won't be attacked."

Most of us aren't trained to think in positive terms, especially when it comes to negative forces. Unfortunately, if you program your crystals against negativity, you could be setting yourself up for more of the same. In fact, when you focus on darkness, rather than light, you could be stirring up a cloud of psychic dust and debris that will swirl around you indefinitely. You could actually find that you are inadvertently broadcasting negative energy back out in the world—and your signals will almost certainly be picked up by anyone who might be tuned into that frequency. In a worst-case scenario, you could even be acting like a beacon to predators . . . the type of people who can smell blood in the water, sense your weakness, and simply add to your problems.

While it might sound like superstition, there is a valid metaphysical principle to remember: like attracts like. There's also a psychological component to consider—if all of your attention is focused on dark issues, when will you find the time or opportunity to focus on lighter, brighter issues? If you're thinking only of all the bad things that could happen, will you even be able to notice any good fortune and opportunity that comes your way?

Don't cower in fear—concentrate on freedom, instead. Don't focus on protection—concentrate on pleasure. Don't worry about what you could lose—simply enjoy what you have. Program your crystals to help you be as positive as possible.

Envision yourself living the life you want—happy, healthy, secure, energetic, and surrounded by love and affection. Program your crystals for what you *do* want, and avoid imbuing them with *don'ts.*

You can program your crystals to help you feel safer and more secure. But if you really are in danger, call a locksmith or call the police. You need to protect yourself with more than a shiny piece of quartz or a few grains of salt.

Active and Reflective

Crystal Meditation

When René Descartes wrote his groundbreaking *Meditations*, he coined one of the most famous expressions in all of Western philosophy: "I think, therefore I am."

The very act of thinking, he postulated, proves that we exist. Granted, he said, we can doubt our senses, and we can doubt what our senses tell us about the world. As a result, we can doubt the reality of the world, and we can certainly doubt the existence of God. But there is no way to doubt that some kernel of our being is thinking about all we have to doubt, and that leads to one inescapable conclusion: we exist, even if nothing else does.

Happily, Descartes went on to demonstrate that if we exist, the rest of the world exists, as well, so we don't have to worry about suddenly finding ourselves as lost, disembodied intelligences floating through the empty void of space.

While meditation can prove that you're alive, it can also enhance the quality of your life. Meditating for just ten minutes a day will lower your heart rate, your blood pressure, and your cholesterol. You will feel calmer, more optimistic, and less anxious or fearful. You will learn faster, and remember what you have learned over longer periods of time. You will be less prone to illness and infection—and you'll look and feel younger, too.

Basic Crystal Meditation

Before you start meditating, make sure you're in a quiet place where you won't be interrupted. Find a comfortable sitting position, either in a chair or on the ground. Some people like to sit on a small pillow. You can lie down, if you're not too tired—but be careful not to fall asleep. Have a blanket handy, because after a few minutes of sitting still you might feel cold. If you are just learning how to meditate with crystals, plan to try it for just ten or fifteen minutes at a time.

Get comfortable, and pick up one of your favorite crystals. Examine it closely; look at every side, every angle, every facet and crevice. Run your fingers over its surface, and feel its weight in your hand.

Then close your eyes, and repeat the process. This time, explore the crystal with your hands while you visualize the stone in your mind's eye. Be open to any impressions you get from the crystal. They may be visual. You might "see" images of people, places, or things in your mind's eye. You might "hear" something—a short sentence, a snippet of conversation, or a line from a favorite song might suddenly pop into your head. You might feel a temperature change.

You might smell flowers, or hear birds, taste salty sea air, or sense a cool breeze moving across your skin. You might even feel emotions that seem to come out of nowhere and catch you by surprise.

Most people say the experiences they have while holding crystals are positive. Those experiences vary in intensity. Some are subtle, consisting of little more than a gentle sense of relaxation or a slight boost in energy. Others report feeling as though they have been taken somewhere else in place or time, with a detailed awareness of the new world around them.

If you don't like your experience, you can stop it at any point; just open your eyes and put the crystal away. But if you like the experience—as most people do—you can recreate it whenever you wish, simply by picking up your crystal and settling down for a few more minutes of meditation.

Expanding Your Practice

Try the following crystal meditation exercises, designed to help you with two varieties of meditation: active, in which you keep your body busy so your mind can wander, and reflective, in which you quiet both your body and your mind.

Start and finish each session with a few minutes of deep breathing. When you're through, record your insights and observations in your crystals journal.

Reflective Meditation

Reflective meditation is calming, quiet, and passive. For Westerners, it comes closest to Zen meditation, in which the goal is to forget oneself and experience the universe as a whole. Here are some reflective meditations that you can try.

Rise and fall. Lie on your back, and put a crystal on your chest or stomach. Watch the crystal rise and fall as you breathe slowly in and out.

Sit still. Sit barefoot, with the soles of your feet pressed together. Balance a crystal on your head, or balance crystals on your shoulders or your knees. Sit still, and focus only on maintaining your balance so the crystals don't fall off.

Get to the point. Hold a quartz point to help you focus during meditation, especially if there is a pressing issue you want to think about.

Quantum leaps. While crystals certainly feel solid in your hand, spend some time imagining them on a quantum level. Feel your consciousness shrink to a subatomic level, where you can feel molecules vibrate and atoms dance to the cosmic rhythm of the universe. Picture yourself as energy, pure and simple, flowing freely in the open areas of the crystal's atomic lattice and molecular framework. Imagine yourself as a particle, a neuron, or a quark, moving through the endless spiral dance of time and space.

Mix and match. Hold a dark crystal in one hand and a light crystal in the other. Imagine the energy rising from each one in waves of colored light, swirling and blending around you, until you feel balanced.

Color breathing. Choose a brightly colored crystal, or one with a hue that you find especially healing, soothing, or intriguing. As you hold the crystal, imagine that it is filling the air around you with its color, tinting the air with subtle tints and hues. Breathe deeply and imagine that color filling your body, oxygenating your bloodstream, moving and circulating with every breath you take and every beat of your heart. Imbue yourself from head to toe with the healing qualities of the color you hold in your hand. When you're finished, allow the atmosphere around you to return to its normal state before you head back into your regular routine.

Moving pictures. Choose a crystal with a flat, smooth side. Imagine that as you gaze at the flat side of the stone, it starts to glow, like a projection screen. Allow images and scenes from your life to be played out on the screen, as if you were watching a movie. Be open to any visions that take shape, even if they unfold only in your mind's eye.

Go inside. Pick up a crystal and study it carefully. Look for inclusions—trace elements of other minerals, rainbows, or veils—and notice any cracks or chips. You might feel as though you are peering into another world. You might see buildings, or landscapes, or the faces or silhouettes of people, animals, and mythical creatures.

Then imagine yourself growing smaller, or visualize the crystal growing larger. Imagine what it would be like to enter the crystal, and walk through it as if it were a great crystal cavern. Explore all of the fissures and crevices. Watch the interplay of light and shadow as sun or moonbeams bounce off its facets and travel through the stone. Enjoy your visit to a timeless world, one that was created long before you were born and will continue to exist long after you leave.

Rock on. As you hold a crystal in your hand, imagine that you *are* the crystal. Picture your early stages of development, first as molten magma, flowing freely within the earth, and then as a seed crystal, deep within the earth's crust. Experience your growth as a crystal, in the dark chambers of an ancient continent, evolving slowly and silently through thousands of years. Imagine what it was like to be discovered, mined, and lifted to the surface of the earth. Then visualize your journey to the place where you now sit—passed from hand to hand, packaged and shipped, dusted and put on display—all along its path to you.

Crystal deva meditation. Hold a crystal in your hand. It can be any crystal—unpolished specimen or tumbled stone, carved totem or crystal rune, large stone or small. Imagine the crystal getting warmer and warmer to your touch. Feel it begin to tingle, and then to vibrate, as a white light begins to glow deep within the crystal.

As the white light begins to spread, it changes color— from red, to orange, yellow, green, blue, indigo, and violet.

The rainbow hues slowly come together in the shape of a graceful arc, which moves from the crystal in your hand to a space about three feet in front of you.

That rainbow will become a bridge, and the ethereal spirit of the crystal deva will travel out from the crystal into the real world. Breathe deeply, and he or she will materialize right before your very eyes.

Picture the deva taking shape in front of you. Visualize every detail of his or her physical appearance: size, shape, color, clothing, hair, and expression. Ask the deva for a message, and listen quietly for a response. You might only receive a nod, a cryptic one- or two-word answer, or an emotion in response—or you may be able to engage the crystal deva in a full-fledged conversation.

Active Meditation

Active meditation is dynamic and lively; it usually involves physical movement. Here are some active meditations that you can try.

Rock walks. Take a walk, and keep your eyes open for new crystals and stones to add to your collection. You are likely to find quartz in its raw, natural form around rivers and streams, for example, and rocks like feldspar and granite in fields and unpaved roads.

Target practice. Hold a crystal in your left hand, and point at it with the index finger of your right hand. Imagine a beam of pure white light flowing into your body from the sky above your head, its source high in the upper reaches of our atmosphere. Then imagine that you can release a continuous stream of that energy through the tip of your index finger. Aim your finger at the crystal in your hand, and imagine your energy flowing into the stone.

You might want to set up a feedback loop, in which a second stream of energy will flow from the crystal back in your direction. Traditionally, the right hand is used to send energy, while the left hand is used to receive.

You can put the crystal down on a table or the floor and practice sending and receiving energy from various distances. You can also practice controlling and releasing that energy from each of your fingers in turn, or from both of your hands, or your third eye, or from any of your chakras.

Remember to switch off the flow of energy when you're through playing . . . and if you plan to aim your cosmic guns at anything but crystals, be sure you don't point at anything you don't intend to shoot.

Crystal milestones. Choose a crystal to represent each major milestone of your life so far. As you choose your crystals, try to develop a rationale to explain each choice; you might choose a white stone to represent the innocence of your early years, for example, or a red stone to symbolize the passion of your youth, and a green stone for your first forays into the working world. Be as specific and detailed as possible, and lay the stones in a design or pattern of your choice.

Stone goalposts. Choose a crystal to represent goals for the next week, the next month, and the next year. Program those crystals with your intentions, and keep them around as a tangible reminder of your hopes and dreams and the steps you need to take to make your vision a reality.

Crystal mandalas. Use crystals to create a mandala—a colorful, circular design that represents the shape and the creation of the universe. Mandalas incorporate precise geometric patterns, which makes it easy to visualize energy flowing in and out of their construction. You can construct your mandala of uncut and unpolished gems, tumbled stones, quartz points, or any crystals in your collection.

The colors of consciousness. As you experiment with crystal meditation, try choosing stones based on a color wheel. A color wheel will show you the three primary colors— red, yellow, and blue—that can't be mixed from other colors. It will show you the three secondary colors—green, orange, and violet—that result when you mix primary colors. And it will show you tertiary colors—like blue-green, red-violet, and yellow-green—that are created when you mix primary colors with secondary colors.

Colors directly opposite each other on the color wheel are complimentary colors. Use complimentary colors when you want to find balance in your work with crystals.

To balance the energies represented by red crystals— such as anger or passion—use green. To bring new energy into a life that feels too sedate—or blue—use orange crystals. If you are feeling too intellectual—which is classically

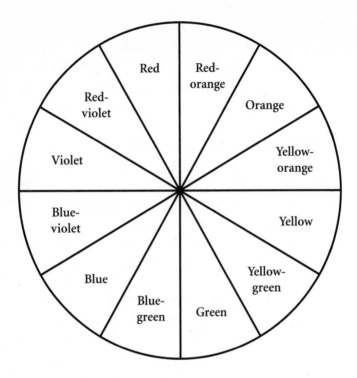

symbolized by the color yellow—pull in some energy from a spiritual purple stone.

You can also try mixing the energies of secondary and tertiary colors simply by determining what each color symbolizes in your own life. The possibilities are as endless as the paint combinations on an artist's palette.

Sixth Sense

*Psychic Development
and Divination*

Crystals are inextricably linked with divination—which, simply put, is contact with the divine. There are many forms of crystal divination: you can scry with a classic crystal ball, or try your hand at rune casting. You can also use crystals as an adjunct to related fields, such as tarot cards, astrological counseling, and psychic readings.

Before you start dabbling in divination, however, it's always a good idea to ensure that you're working with positive forces, and that your own mood is as light, positive, and optimistic as possible.

Before you begin any psychic work, you might want to add a few drops of crystal elixir to a full eight-ounce glass of water. (You can find the directions for concocting a crystal elixir in the chapter called "Feeling Good.") Water is associated with psychic ability and intuition for a reason: on a physical and mental level, water helps ensure that your cells are chemically balanced and fully charged. On a spiritual

NORTHERN LIGHTS LIBRARY SYSTEM
POSTAL BAG 8
ELK POINT, ALBERTA
T0A 1A0

and emotional level, water helps psychic impressions flow freely.

Many psychics start their sessions with a few moments of cleansing, centering, grounding, and shielding. If you don't have a starting routine of your own, just breathe deeply, put both feet on the floor, envision yourself surrounded by pure, white light, and say the following words:

I am protected, day and night,
By a circle of white light.
No evil may enter or even draw near,
For peace and goodness keep me here.

As you work, continue to visualize yourself surrounded by a protective shield of white light. You can visualize a crystal as a focal point for that light.

Whenever you are dealing with outside sources of information, remember to ground and protect yourself with that shield of pure white light.

Remember, too, that you don't need to afford your psychic sources of information any more credit than you would give to a close, trusted friend—especially if you don't have a long history of working with a particular spirit guide. Advice is cheap, even in the spirit world. Ultimately, you are responsible for making your own choices, and you will be the one who has to live with the consequences of any decision you make.

Back and Forth

If you want to know which way the winds of change are blowing, you might want to try your hand at pendulum dowsing.

A pendulum can be any object on a string—rings, a bead, a button—but some of the most impressive pendulums are crafted from crystals.

Crystal pendulums are typically drilled or glued so they can be suspended from a chain, or wrapped with wire so they can be suspended from a ribbon or a velvet cord. They're beautiful, and they have a huge advantage over pendulums crafted from manufactured materials: crystal pendulums come with built-in strengths, straight from the natural world. If you know what type of questions you will probably ask, you can even choose crystal pendulums that correlate to those subject areas. If you want to dowse for information about relationships, for example, try a pendulum made from a pink-colored crystal, like rose quartz. If you want to dowse about money issues, try a green-colored crystal, like aventurine or moss agate. If you want to use your pendulum to augment your other psychic tools, such as tarot cards or runes, try an amethyst pendulum.

You can find pendulums in any metaphysical shop, and they're usually very affordable—so you can add several to your collection. Ultimately, however, you only really need one pendulum—and if you want a good, all-purpose pendulum, clear quartz is always a good choice.

A nineteenth-century scientist named Michel Eugene Chevreul demonstrated that pendulums move in response to involuntary muscle movements—imperceptible twitches and tics that come about as a result of passing thoughts and hopeful wishes. Anyone who argues that science negates the effectiveness of pendulum dowsing, however, is missing the point. A pendulum is a remarkable tool for picking up, tuning in, and amplifying messages and information from your subconscious mind.

To try pendulum dowsing for yourself, first make sure that you are attuned to your pendulum. Hold the chain, ribbon, or cord between your thumb and index finger so that the pendulum dangles about six inches below your hand.

Make sure the pendulum is motionless, and then ask it—silently or with spoken words—to show you which direction it will move for "yes" and which way it will swing for "no."

Experiment with holding it in both your right hand and your left hand. If you are normally right-handed, hold it in your left, which is generally considered to represent your intuitive, receptive side. On the other hand—literally—you might find that it's easier for you to hold it steady in your rational, right hand.

You can use a pendulum to answer direct, yes-or-no questions. Look directly down at a pendulum, and it will indicate its response in one of several ways:

- Yes—up and down, like someone nodding his head.
- No—back and forth, like someone shaking his head from side to side.

- Maybe—a diagonal movement from the lower left to the upper right.
- Don't want to answer—a diagonal swing from the lower right to the upper left.
- Probably—a clockwise circle.
- Probably not—a counter-clockwise circle.

Once you and your pendulum are synchronized, you can begin to divine with it.

If you have a question, ask it aloud. You should be very specific in how you phrase your inquiry. "Should I invite Kim to the ball game tomorrow?" will get you a clearer answer than "Should I ask Kim on a date?"

You can also write your question on a piece of paper, with "yes" in one corner and "no" in the other, so your pendulum can point you in the right direction. In fact, you can develop a simple, all-purpose diagram with the words "yes," "no," and "maybe."

You can even make or find a full-fledged pendulum board with words, numbers, and images designed to reveal the answers you seek or enhance the answers you receive. Professionally designed boards usually include the words "yes" and "no," along with numbers, letters of the alphabet, and sometimes the days of the week, months, or seasons of the year.

Pendulums aren't limited to simple yes-and-no questions. If you are looking for lost objects, hold your pendulum over a map of the area in which you are searching. If you are trying to set a date for an important event, hold your pendulum over a calendar.

You can use a pendulum to help you with any psychic project. You can use a pendulum to help you choose which crystals to buy or use. You can use a pendulum in your crystal healing sessions to help you determine which areas of the body need special attention. You can even use a crystal pendulum in conjunction with channeling to make it easier for your spirit guides to communicate with you. And you can also use a pendulum to augment your other tools. Using a pendulum is one way to choose cards for a tarot reading, for example.

Pendulums are a lot of fun, and they're a great way to set foot in the psychic realm.

Gaze into My Crystal Ball

*Scrying, Channeling,
and Crystalomancy*

Everyone has seen gypsies and fortunetellers in movies or on television gazing into their crystal balls and making astounding predictions and pronouncements.

While we all wish we could peek into a crystal ball and catch a glimpse of the future, that's not quite how it works in real life. Sadly, you may never be able to wave your hand and see a photographic image of the tall dark stranger that's headed your way.

However, you can use crystal orbs and spheres for both meditation and divination. The process is called scrying or crystalomancy.

Contrary to popular belief, you don't need a big crystal ball on the center of your table. For one thing, real crystal balls carved from a solid piece of crystal can be prohibitively expensive. While less expensive versions are available, they are usually glass or lead crystal, made from melted, ground-up quartz.

For crystal gazing, you simply need a genuine, natural crystal that's at least two inches (or about 50 millimeters) in diameter, which would also be about six inches (or 160 millimeters) in circumference. That's just slightly bigger than a golf ball.

You don't need a perfectly round crystal ball. Instead, you might prefer to work with an egg-shaped crystal, a large oval, a pyramid, or even a mirrorlike crystal slab.

You don't need a perfectly clear crystal ball, either. In fact, a crystal with veils, rainbows, and inclusions could actually work better than a clear crystal because you'll have more of a starting point for your visions.

Believe it or not, you don't even need a quartz crystal. Any type of crystal will help you focus your awareness and slip into a meditative state.

Ultimately, choosing a crystal ball may be the most difficult part of scrying. Once you have the right tool, the rest is easy.

First, cleanse and charge your crystal ball as you would any other crystal in your collection.

Then clear a space where you can work in peace and in privacy, uninterrupted by ringing telephones or curious passersby. Make sure the area is neat and clean, too, so you won't be distracted by clutter or the reminder of work you need to do.

Dim the lights. If direct sunlight is coming in through the windows, pull the shade or close the drapes. Your goal should be to eliminate any bright reflections in your ball.

Light a white candle to draw pure and protective energy into the room, but don't put it so close to the crystal that you can see its reflection.

Sit with both feet firmly on the floor. Take several deep breaths, in through your nose and out through your mouth.

You may hold your crystal ball in your hands, if you like, or position it on a cushion or a table stand.

Imagine the space around you and the crystal ball filling with clear, white light.

Gaze steadily into the ball. Let your eyes go slightly out of focus, as if you were daydreaming; don't squint or strain to see into the crystal. Simply look at the ball, relaxing deeper and deeper with each breath, and let the visions come to you.

At first, a cloudy mist might seem to fill the crystal, or some parts of the ball might seem to shimmer and fill with light. If the crystal has inclusions, they might seem to move, just a little, or shift in size and shape. You might even start to see visions and images, as if you were paging through a photo album or watching a movie on a metaphysical screen.

Don't be discouraged, however, if the experience is something less than earth-shaking—especially at first. In fact, it's very likely that your first few efforts at crystal gazing will result in a series of more subdued psychic impressions. You might not see anything in the crystal, for example, but you might see an image in your mind's eye. A word, a sentence, a phrase, or a snippet of song might pop into your head, seemingly out of nowhere. You might sense a change in temperature, or feel a breeze move softly across your skin. You might smell flowers, or fruit, or perfume. You might even get a flash of insight or understanding into a problem or situation you have been dealing with for some time.

Just as you experience the physical world through a wide range of senses and experiences, you can experience the psychic world through an entire host of occurrences, too. Crystals and crystal balls can help you tap into and develop your psychic abilities, no matter what form they take.

If you are just starting to learn crystalomancy, spend only five or ten minutes on your first few sessions, and gradually build up your focus and concentration. After each session, record the date and a few notes about your experience in your crystals journal, and then put your crystal ball away for safekeeping.

According to tradition, crystal balls should never be exposed to direct sunlight, and they should be covered with black velvet or black silk when they're not in use. Sunlight, some people say, will drain a crystal ball of its power—but the real reason for keeping a crystal ball covered could simply be pragmatic. When the sun's rays pass through a clear crystal ball, they could easily start a fire. You can choose for yourself whether you want to keep your crystal ball covered, but don't store it on a stack of old newspapers, and don't keep it next to the kindling in your fireplace.

Friends in High Places

While channeling—the act of connecting with the spiritual realm—might sound a little spooky at first, most people have had channeling experiences without even realizing it. You may have been asleep, but you woke suddenly with the solution to a problem that had been nagging you for days. You may have written a story or a poem without much conscious thought or effort—words simply seemed to flow from the tip of your pen. Someone may have asked you a difficult question, and you blurted the correct response without even thinking.

Ultimately, channeling simply describes the act of making contact or communicating with spirit, whether you perceive that spirit in the form of guides, guardian angels, the holy spirit, God, or simply your own higher self.

Crystals can help you slip into a meditative state where you can channel information quickly, easily, and readily, from any source. One type of crystal—a channeling crystal—is said to be especially good for helping people connect with outside sources of information.

Channeling crystals are clear quartz crystals that typically have at least one large seven-sided face on one side of their tip, and a triangular, three-sided face on the other. Some channeling crystals are also ordinary pieces of clear quartz wrapped in copper wire.

If you want to try channeling with your crystal, start by cleansing and clearing it.

Then clear a space where you can work in peace and in privacy, uninterrupted by ringing telephones or curious passersby. Make sure the area is neat and clean, too, so you won't be distracted.

Dim the lights, and sit in a comfortable chair with both of your feet planted firmly on the floor, for grounding.

Hold your channeling crystal in your hands and breathe deeply. As you look at the crystal, envision the space around you filling with a spiral-shaped column of bright, white light, energizing and uplifting you as it swirls in a clockwise direction around you.

Then imagine that the spirit guide you wish to talk with is in that light, and that he or she will slowly materialize before your very eyes.

The spirit might not be what you expect. It could come to you in the form of a man or a woman, but it could just as easily manifest as a small spirit animal, a devalike elf or fairy, a cluster of sparkling lights, a swirl of color, a wisp of smoke, or simply an invisible presence and a still, small voice inside your head. It could materialize in front of you, or you might see it only within the confines of the crystal itself. When you work with a channeling crystal, you should try to remain open to any possibility.

If you have trouble envisioning such a development in your own home, try to set the stage by imagining yourself in the spirit world instead. As you breathe deeply and gaze into your channeling crystal, picture yourself sitting with the crystal in a quiet park, in a peaceful meadow, or on a tropical beach at sunset—anywhere you would feel calm, comfortable, and relaxed. In the garden of your mind's eye, you might have an easier time allowing your channeled experiences to unfold.

Feel free to ask direct questions, and expect to receive straight answers in response. You can ask them aloud, or just pose them silently in your thoughts. You could even prepare one main inquiry in advance of your channeling session, and write it down on a piece of paper.

The information you receive could come in the form of images, symbols, thoughts, or feelings. It could be as clear as crystal, or cloudy and confusing. Either way, don't try to second-guess or rationalize the information you receive during a channeling session. Simply acknowledge it, thank the source, and conclude the session by visualizing all of the white light flowing down into your crystal.

Record your experiences in your crystals journal so you can refer back to it as events unfold. Then ground yourself with a few deep breaths, get up, and resume your day.

Even if you think the information you received actually comes from your subconscious mind, you will still be channeling energy from a higher source.

You shouldn't feel tired or drained after a channeling session. If you do, spend more time grounding yourself, and picture white light coming from the space around you, not your own body.

Like any metaphysical practice, your channeling sessions will get easier and more interesting with time. Experiment as often as you like.

Crystals and Psychic Readings

You can use crystals alone to conduct psychic readings, or you can use crystals to augment other types of divination. Here are some practical tips to incorporate them into a larger metaphysical practice:

- Use crystals to cleanse and clear your tarot cards: simply store your cards with the crystal of your choice.

- When you give tarot readings or astrological reports to other people, give them a crystal to hold. Some people are a little nervous during a reading; holding a crystal will help ground them. Some people are also a little scattered; a crystal can help them focus and listen to the information you present.

- When you finish your sessions with other people, give them a small crystal or a tumbled stone to keep, to help them remember the experience.

Sweet Dreams

The Twilight World of
Crystals After Hours

Most people need at least seven hours of sleep every night. That means that someone who lives to be seventy-seven—the average life span in the United States—will have spent more than twenty-two years asleep.

That time isn't wasted—much of it is spent in dreams, where we can live parallel lives and experience wonders we could never imagine during our waking hours.

Psychologists are often fascinated by dreams. Sigmund Freud once theorized that dreams were the royal road to the unconscious mind, where each of us could excavate the unresolved conflicts of our lives. Carl Jung believed that dreams allow us to tap into the collective unconscious, a psychic reservoir of shared experiences and archetypal imagery. Fritz Perls, the father of Gestalt therapy, theorized that everything in a dream is actually a reflection of the dreamer, and that understanding dream symbols could lead to a healthier, more integrated life.

Dreams can also be a wellspring of inspiration, ideas, messages, and signs—and you can use crystals to pave the royal road to your unconscious mind.

Sweet dreams. If you simply want to generate good dreams for yourself or a loved one, put a small blue stone under your pillow or a larger blue crystal under your bed. Use crystals that reflect the colors of night and the midnight sky. Try sodalite, for the look of clean white clouds under a full moon; lapis lazuli, which looks like fireworks in an evening sky; or black onyx, for the midnight depths of another world.

Lucid dreams. For lucid dreams, in which you are aware of the fact that you're dreaming and you control the course of events in your dreams, tape a crystal to your third-eye chakra in the middle of your forehead. Try, if you can, to be aware of that crystal even as you sleep, to remind you to take control and make decisions in your dreams.

Dream recall. If you want to remember your dreams, program a crystal to record your impressions and experiences, and keep it on your nightstand. You will have even better luck remembering your dreams if you use that crystal in conjunction with a written record of your dreams.

Before you go to bed, open your crystals journal and write, "Tonight, I will dream, and I will remember my dreams." Leave the pen handy, so you can write down your recollections as soon as you wake up from a dream, before you come to complete consciousness.

Also, make sure there is a low-watt bulb in your bedside lamp, so that you won't have to get out of bed to turn on a light, and so that the light won't be so bright that it shocks you into full alertness.

Bad dreams. If you are troubled by bad dreams or nightmares, create a grid of crystals around your bed to catch and entrap any negative images. Stones with naturally occurring holes are also said to help prevent nightmares.

Crystal dream pillows. Years ago, women created scented dream pillows for every member of the family, designed to lull them to sleep with the sweet scent of flower petals and essential oils. Add a few tiny crystals to your handcrafted dream pillows, and you are practically guaranteed a pleasant journey into the land of Nod.

Dream pillows are easy enough for children to make. The seams don't need to be perfectly straight—dream pillows are designed to be charming, after all, in the truest sense of the word. You also don't have to worry about making them perfectly smooth or perfectly plump; they are intended to supplement your regular pillow, not to replace it.

To make a dream pillow, find two pieces of soft fabric, six to twelve inches square. Pin the two pieces together, inside out. Sew the fabric together on three sides, but leave one side open so you can add stuffing. Remove the pins and turn the pillow right side out, so the seams are on the inside. Fill it with stuffing, but leave a little nest in the center for your herb and crystal insert. (If you are really pressed for time, you can also use a ready-made pillow from a store, and simply open the seam enough to insert your herbs and crystals.)

For the insert, use a piece of mesh or muslin fabric. Lay the mesh or muslin flat, and create a little mound of rose petals, lavender buds, calendula, or chamomile. You can also add mugwort, cinnamon, or marjoram spices, if you like. Activate the dried herbs with a few drops of soothing essential oil—lavender, peppermint, rose, or eucalyptus oil are all good choices. Then add one, two, or three very small, very smooth tumbled stones or crystals of your choice. Tie the insert closed with a piece of ribbon, and tuck it into the nest in the center of the pillow. Add a little more stuffing—but don't pack it too tightly, because air needs to circulate through the pillow in order for scent to be released.

Periodically, you can open your pillow and add a few more drops of essential oil to reinvigorate the scent.

Sweet dreams!

Flying High

Crystals and Astral Travel

If you like to travel—or if you just need to get out of the house more—crystals could be your ticket to the astral plane.

Astral travel is a meditative exercise, a lot like lucid dreaming. During astral travel, your consciousness leaves your body and travels through space and time in the astral plane, a spiritual level of reality filled with thoughts and mental imagery.

Astral travel is accomplished mostly through creative visualization, bordering on wild flights of fancy and creative imagination. If you would like to try it, your crystals can help speed you on your way.

Any crystal that soothes, calms, or helps you slip into a meditative state can give you a boost into the astral plane. Stones that are associated with the skies and the heavens seem especially appropriate—try angelite, apophyllite, celestite, iolite, moonstone, selenite, and seraphinite. Crystals with meteoric origins, like moldavite and tektite, can also help carry you magically into other planes of existence and other worlds. You might even like to try holding mochi marbles, which are sometimes called shaman stones.

To begin your astral travels, find a quiet time when you can lie down on your bed. Close your door and unplug the phone, so you won't be interrupted by family members, phone calls, or unexpected visitors.

Then select a destination. You might want to start small—choose the neighborhood where you grew up, or the home of a close friend, or a shopping center across town. If you're feeling a little more daring, you might want to visit a tourist resort or a scenic area in a foreign land. (You are traveling, after all.)

Write your destination on an index card or a piece of paper, and place it, face up, on your bed or on your nightstand. Later, if you are surprised to find yourself looking at it from a spot near your bedroom ceiling, you'll remember where you're supposed to go.

If you worry about leaving your body behind, you can create a protective grid out of the crystals of your choice. You can even fashion a "landing strip" for your reentry out of clear quartz stones and quartz tips and points.

Lie down on your bed, flat on your back, with a crystal in each hand. Remember that dark stones like obsidian and hematite will usually be grounding, while light stones like clear quartz and selenite will often help you reach new heights of spirituality. You might also want to put a crystal on your psychic third eye, right in the middle of your forehead. If you have butterflies in your stomach, put a crystal on your solar plexus.

Close your eyes. Breathe deeply and relax completely, starting with your feet and progressing all the way to your head.

Picture yourself in your mind's eye. Visualize yourself lying there, in as much detail as you can muster.

Then imagine your psychic self, floating two or three feet above your physical body, as comfortably as if you were resting on an air mattress on a lake or a pool.

Some people say they hear loud noises when they first leave their bodies, like a howling wind or the music of a cosmic orchestra. Don't panic and dive back in to your physical form; just take a deep psychic breath, and the noise will quiet down.

From your position in midair, look down at your physical self, and then look around the room you are in. Look for the note you left to remind yourself of your destination, and practice moving in your psychic body. Use your arms and legs to propel yourself forward and back, just as if you were swimming or flying through the air.

Then imagine yourself floating comfortably through the ceiling or out your bedroom window.

Enjoy a bird's-eye view of your home, your backyard, and your neighborhood, and then head for the destination you had in mind when you initiated your out-of-body experience. You might find yourself traveling through the air, or you might find yourself transported there instantly.

Feel free to look around and explore.

When you are ready to go home, imagine yourself back in your room, still floating a few feet above your physical body. If you set up a crystal shield or landing strip, admire your handiwork and get your bearings.

Then allow yourself to ease back into your body. Feel the crystals in your hands, and take a few deep breaths to reintegrate your body and soul and come back to full consciousness.

Record your experiences and your insights in your crystals journal.

Practical Magic

Crystal Affirmations and Spells

Crystals have their own inherent power to inspire, to guide, and to transform reality. When you add your own magic to the mix—in the form of good intentions, life-altering affirmations, and old-fashioned "wishcraft"—you might find that you have the power to change the world.

Magical Realism

Before you start casting spells and enchanting everyone you meet, a few precautions are in order. You truly can work magic with the power of your thoughts, words, and deeds—but when you add crystal clarity and focus to your actions, you might get more than you bargained for. In fact, the process is so powerful that practitioners of practical magic have developed some guidelines for beginners.

First, do what you can to accomplish your goals without resorting to crystal magic. If you want a new job, polish up your resume and start sending it out. If you're hoping to find love, get a good haircut and learn how to dance. If you want to lose weight, spend more time walking than watching TV. Direct action is always the most effective way to change your life.

Once you decide to augment your own efforts with crystal magic, make sure that your intentions are good. Then build a fail-safe into all of your work, because you can't always see all of the ramifications of all of your actions.

Don't try to use practical magic to hurt anyone—any negativity you put out into the world will probably come back to bite you in the end, and you'll be the one who gets hurt the most.

Don't try to trick other people, either. If you want to catch the eye of a good-looking guy, or sweet-talk a beautiful woman into dinner and a movie, use your own charm—not a magic charm. Yes, you can change your luck by charging the environment around you with your thoughts and energy—but you should still be willing to take no for an answer. It's just bad karma to interfere with anyone's free will.

And finally, be careful what you wish for. Once you set a chain of events in motion, it may be impossible to call things to a halt.

Affirmative Action

The easiest spells are affirmations—a form of practical magic that work on both a conscious and subconscious level. In both theory and practice, affirmations retrain your brain. Affirmations also help you think in positive terms, so you can clearly envision yourself living the life of your dreams and focus on your goals.

Add crystal power to your affirmations, and you'll have a tangible reminder to follow through on the affirmations you've developed for yourself.

Affirmations are remarkably simple to devise. First, think of something specific that you want in your life. Don't be too philosophical or abstract; be clear and direct.

Be positive, not negative. If you want to lose weight, focus on the goal weight you want to reach, not the weight you need to lose.

Start small, and you'll see immediate results. Your affirmations can be as practical as "I always remember to change my oil every 3,000 miles" or as simple and uplifting as "I look good in red." Later on, as your life starts to improve, your affirmations can grow in complexity and scope.

Write your affirmations in the present tense, so your mind and spirit can immediately make adjustments in your outlook.

Be specific in the results you hope to achieve, but be open-minded about the means to your end. Don't try to micromanage your own fate—be open to any possibility.

Don't limit yourself by being too stingy in your thinking, either—especially when it comes to prosperity. If you need more cash to pay your bills, choose an affirmation of "plenty," rather than an affirmation of "just enough."

Think long-term. Set goals that could last your whole life long: a loving relationship with another person, money for all the things you need—and want—and a strong, healthy body, so you can live comfortably for many, many years.

Ultimately, you want your affirmations to become part of a permanent mindset, not a temporary phase.

Program your affirmations into a crystal, and then tuck the handwritten affirmation away.

Stars, Moons, Hearts, Clovers

Crystal Lucky Charms

In 2004, when psychologists at the University of Hertford-shire near London studied the effectiveness of lucky charms, they found that good luck tokens really do work—at least in the minds of those who carry them.[1]

In the study, researchers asked a hundred people to carry a Victorian-era penny for a month and note any changes in their lives. Afterward, they tried to determine whether the charms had made any difference, statistically, compared to people who didn't have lucky charms.

Oddly enough, while researchers determined that lucky charms didn't influence chance events like winning the lottery, the participants in the study *felt* luckier. Almost all of them felt more confident, more secure, more optimistic

---

1. Ananova, "Lucky Charm's Effectiveness 'All in the Mind,'" January 5, 2004, http://www.ananova.com/.

about the future. When the study concluded, seventy percent of the participants even chose to keep carrying their lucky pennies.

If you want a psychological boost—and a buffer against the fickle finger of fate—crystals could be your lucky charm.

Amulets and talismans are often thought of synonymously, but there is a subtle difference between them. Amulets are typically out of carved stone, while talismans usually made of engraved metal and ornamented with carved crystals and stones. Amulets are worn for protection; they are intended to keep bad things away. Talismans are worn for luck; they are designed to bring good things to their wearers.

Pocket charms. Small tumbled stones make excellent good luck charms, either tucked into your pocket or carried in a purse. You can even find tumbled stones made into key chains. Chiastolite crystals, commonly known as fairy crosses, are classic lucky charms.

Totems are crystals carved in the shape of an animal or a mythical creature. Totems can symbolize your spirit, your cultural traditions, or your membership in a community. Totems can also lend you the gifts and strengths associated with each shape. A bear-shaped totem, for example, symbolizes maternal instincts and protection. Cats symbolize independence, regal bearing, agility, multiple lives, and magic. Dragons symbolize a fiery spirit, guardianship, and power over obstacles and foes.

Worry stones. If you're the restless, fidgety type, keep a worry stone around. Worry stones are flat, palm-sized stones with a carved groove on one side. Just rub your thumb back and forth in the groove, and you'll turn your nervous energy into good fortune.

Feeling Good

Crystals for Health and Healing

Crystals are sometimes heralded as curing agents for any illness or disease imaginable, from cancer to the common cold. Some crystal healers report astounding success with their clients, who are said to recover from illnesses and crippling conditions after a session or two with the stones.

The best crystal healers, however, are quick to point out one fact that can make crystal healing lose its luster in the bright light of day: crystals, in and of themselves, do not heal anyone. Instead, crystals can serve as a focal point for the healing energy and compassion of caring, sensitive people—and they serve as an even better resource for people who want to kick-start their bodies' own natural healing ability.

A Cautionary Note

Crystals remind us of the beauty and structure of physical life, as well as the spiritual significance we assign to material objects. Crystals can also be used as a focal point for inspiration and enlightenment, and they can prompt us to think and live in healthier ways. They can even be used as conduits for healing energy.

Crystals can be a valuable addition to your health care regimen—but they are *not* a substitute for professional medical advice, diagnosis, or treatment. If you have a medical problem, or you suspect that you have a medical problem, you should consult a qualified healthcare provider.

Healing Yourself

Before you ever begin to try healing others with crystals, learn how crystals can help you heal yourself.

Start by working with just one or two crystals. Experiment with placing them on your trouble spots—your sore ankle or your bad knee, or that muscle on the back of your neck that tenses up when you're under stress. You can even use gentle fabric tape to adhere them to your skin. You can also try using crystals to move energy in the space around your body. Or you can dive right in and try a full-fledged healing session. Just make sure you practice all of the techniques yourself before you try them on another person.

A Typical Healing Session, Step by Step

First, clear a space where you can work in peace and in privacy, uninterrupted by ringing telephones or curious passersby.

Make sure there is room to lie down and stretch out. If you're going to be working with another person, make sure there's room for both of you to move around. You might want to work in a bedroom, assuming you can stand on either side of the bed, or clear a space on the living room floor.

If you want to lie on the floor, put a mat or a soft blanket down first. Have a few throw pillows handy; most people need a pillow under their heads in order to lie comfortably, and many appreciate a pillow or two under their knees, as well.

Dress—and have the other person dress—in comfortable, loose-fitting clothes. A plain white T-shirt and a pair of ordinary black shorts are ideal, because they will allow you to move and the colors won't interfere with the colors of the crystals. If one of your friends does show up for a healing session in a tie-dyed shirt or zebra-striped slacks, have a plain white sheet handy that you can drape across him.

It's important to note that most crystal healing sessions don't involve any sort of massage, and even ordinary touching is limited to putting crystals on and taking them off. For your own safety and legal protection, make sure that all of the people you work with remain fully clothed.

Before you begin, clean the space you will be using, both physically and psychically. Obviously, you will probably want to dust, vacuum, and put away any clutter. If there is a trash can in the room, move it or empty it. Open the windows and fill the room with fresh air. Then visualize the room filling with pure, white light, clearing away any cosmic cobwebs and chasing out any dark shadows that have set up camp in the corner.

To enhance the atmosphere further, you can burn scented candles or incense. If you have a stereo handy, turn on some soft background music.

Bring your crystals into the room, and make sure that they are clean, clear, and fully charged.

You should program your healing crystals in advance. Hold them in your hands, breathe deeply, and visualize them filling with pure, healing energy. Consciously make it clear that their role will be to assist with the healing process in the session to come.

You should also ensure that you have programmed all of the crystals you will be using to do no harm. That way, if they're not the right crystals for the job, they won't do any damage; they will simply remain inert.

Once you're ready to begin, spend the first part of the session simply thinking about the healing work at hand— or if you will be conducting the session on behalf of another person, spend that time talking together.

Physical health will obviously be part of the conversation, but in crystal healing sessions, that discussion will also serve as a gateway to a far broader exchange about spiritual, mental, and emotional well-being.

You can use a series of standard questions to start a conversation with someone who wants a crystal healing session—even if you are only treating yourself. If you are working on your own health issues, write your answers in your crystals journal.

- Why did you come? Why do you want to try a crystal healing session?

- Why did you choose to come now, as opposed to last week, last month, or some time in the future?

- What is your most pressing health concern?

- Is it mostly physical, spiritual, emotional, or intellectual?

- If you are experiencing a health problem, how did it start?

- What have you tried to cure it or heal it so far?

- How satisfied have you been with the results?

- What other measures have you thought about trying?

- Have you done any work with crystals before?

- What do you know about crystals?

- Do you have any reservations or concerns about working with crystals?

- What do you hope you will get from a crystal healing session?

Open your healing session by sitting in silence for a few moments. Hold a favorite crystal in your hands, for grounding and stability, and breathe deeply—in through your nose and out through your mouth. As you breathe, progressively relax all the muscles of your body, starting with your feet and moving all the way to your head. If you are working with someone else, make sure that person is lying down, and guide him or her through progressive relaxation.

Rub your hands briskly together to sensitize them to the auric energy field around the human body. Then run your hands slowly across that field, without touching the body itself. Keep your hands three or four inches away from the skin.

If you seem to sense any areas where energy doesn't seem to be flowing, put a clear quartz crystal on the spot. You will leave it there until it falls off or rolls away on its own accord—a clear signal that its work is done. For long-lasting healing, you can occasionally tape a small, smooth crystal to a trouble spot. Use gentle cloth tape designed to work with bandages so you don't inadvertently inflict more pain on yourself or your long-suffering friends.

Follow your intuition, and experiment with various colors, layouts, and timing techniques.

You can also use crystals as tools to metaphorically sweep away emotional dirt and debris, break through blockages, or absorb negative energy.

Don't be surprised if a crystal healing session seems to bring powerful emotions to the surface. Be willing to end a session whenever you like, but for the most part you should simply know that crying—and a great sense of relief—is normal.

As your healing session draws to a close, use deep breathing to reenergize and reawaken to the everyday world. Spend a few minutes talking about the experience or answering any questions your friend might have.

Make a written record of the crystals you used during each section, along with diagrams of their placement, in your crystals journal.

Clean and clear your crystals, and put them away.

Healing with Light

The easiest way to heal yourself or other people is to use a clear, wand-shaped crystal to visualize white healing light entering your body through the top of your head, then channeling that energy through you and out from the tip of the crystal you hold in your hand.

When you act as a channel for healing energy, rather than a source, you can maintain your own reserves of energy and strength when you're working with other people. You will simply be moving cosmic energy through your body—and possibly getting a boost yourself in the process.

You can also use crystals—of any shape and size—to intuitively sense problem spots, imbalances, and energy blockages, and to move healing energy into and around those areas.

Healing with Color

When you know the special properties of the crystals in your collection—especially the properties based on color—you can consciously select crystals for other people to hold while they talk about their problems and the issues they're facing. The crystals you choose can help them focus, concentrate, communicate, and channel energy into the appropriate sphere.

Color is an important consideration. Each color of crystal incorporates properties that affect us psychologically. You can even give those properties a boost by imagining that the crystals are tinting the air around you. Breathe deeply, and imagine the color filling your body, oxygenating your bloodstream, moving, and circulating, with every breath you take and every beat of your heart. That way, you can imbue yourself from head to toe with the healing qualities of the color you hold in your hand.

White represents spiritual purity, innocence, higher thought, and higher consciousness.

Black, like the earth, is grounding and physical. Use black crystals to stabilize your thoughts, feelings, actions, and emotions, and to feel more in control of your life and health.

Gray, the color of shadows, smoke, and fog, can help you clear away anything that obscures your vision or clouds your outlook.

Red, the color of blood, passion, anger, and alarm, can help you deal with matters of life and death.

Pink is soothing, calming, and peaceful. Use pink crystals for emotional healing.

Orange, the color of spark and flame, can help you feel energetic, vigorous, and alert.

Yellow, like the sun, represents energy and renewal. Yellow is also associated with clarity, logic, and rational thinking.

Green is the color of nature, fertility, and creativity. Use green crystals for renewal, growth, and overall good health.

Blue, the tranquil color of sea and sky, can help you improve your health through relaxation and meditation. You can also use blue crystals to soothe and cool any issues that seem too hot, including physical issues like fevers.

Indigo, the color of the midnight sky, symbolizes deep contemplation, wisdom, self-mastery, and spiritual realization. Use indigo crystals when you want to access cosmic wisdom.

Violet is the color of royalty. Violet once adorned emperors, kings, and queens, and the color represented their leadership and sovereignty over others. As a result, all purple shades connote luxury, wealth, and sophistication.

Brown, the color of the earth, can help you feel more grounded and plant the seeds for better health.

Clear crystals symbolize clarity of thought and vision. Some people believe clear crystals will also amplify the energy and properties of other factors. Use clear crystals when you want to think clearly or focus sharply on any issue.

Rainbow crystals remind us of hope, forgiveness, and the beauty that follows a devastating storm.

Chakra Healing

The word *chakra* is Sanskrit for "wheel" or "disk." The chakras make up the energy system of the human body. Each chakra is associated with a separate area of life. Each one, like a spinning wheel, helps keep energy flowing—spiritually, emotionally, intellectually, and physically. When your chakras are in balance, energy flows freely and you'll feel healthy and strong.

Each chakra is associated with a color, and the colors correspond directly to the rainbow colors of the visible light spectrum: red, orange, yellow, green, blue, indigo, and violet.

Placing colored crystals on the chakras can imbue them with new energy, slow the chakras that are spinning too fast, speed up the chakras that are spinning too slowly, and ultimately help bring all of them into balance.

The first chakra, also known as the base or root chakra, is located at the base of the spine. The first chakra is associated with survival issues, physical existence, and material concerns like food, clothing, and shelter. When the first chakra is blocked or unbalanced, you might feel insecure, fearful, or victimized. Your feet, legs, and lower back might hurt. But when it's balanced, you will feel healthy and strong, eager to get out of bed in the morning and start the day.

The first chakra is red, so you can place red crystals there, like garnets and rubies. But because the first chakra extends down all the way to your feet and the ground that you walk upon, you can also put black and brown crystals there, too, for their grounding qualities. Try hematite, obsidian, or smoky quartz.

Crown

Forehead

Throat

Heart

Solar plexus

Sacral

Base

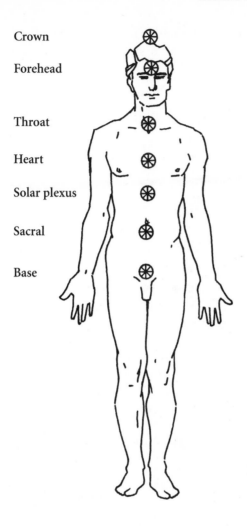

The second chakra, also known as the sacral or spleen chakra, is located midway between your pelvic bone and your navel. The second chakra is associated with sexuality and creativity. When it is blocked or unbalanced, you might feel uninspired. You might suffer from sexual dysfunction, infertility, or circulatory problems. But when it's balanced, you will feel vibrant, alluring, and filled with creative ideas and inspiration.

The second chakra is orange, so you can place orange crystals there. Try garnet, carnelian, tiger's eye, or topaz.

The third chakra, also known as the solar plexus chakra, is located below your breastbone. The third chakra is associated with personal power. When it is blocked or unbalanced, you might feel weak or easily dismayed. You may be overly critical of yourself, or you may be especially vulnerable to criticism and the judgments of others. You may suffer from nervousness and an easily upset stomach. But when it's balanced, you will feel secure in your own abilities, assertive, self-confident, and self-assured.

The third chakra is yellow, so you can use yellow crystals there. Try citrine, fire opal, pyrite, or tiger's eye.

The fourth chakra, also known as the heart chakra, is located right at the level of your heart. The fourth chakra is associated with love and emotion; when it is blocked or unbalanced, you might feel lonely or heartbroken. You may lack compassion for others, or you might be a bleeding heart. You may even experience physical heart conditions. But when the fourth chakra is balanced, you will feel that you deserve to be loved, and you will be able to love others in return. You will be willing to forgive others for old wounds, forgive yourself for past mistakes, and be willing to trust that everything turns out for the best.

The fourth chakra is green, so you can use green crystals there. Bloodstone is especially appropriate; you can also try aventurine, emerald, jade, or malachite. You might also want to experiment with pink-colored crystals, because they are associated with emotional healing and well-being; try rose quartz, pink kunzite, rhodochrosite, or rhodonite.

The fifth chakra, also known as the throat chakra, is located at the level of your throat. The fifth chakra corresponds to your communication skills. When it is blocked or unbalanced, you may feel frustrated and unable to express yourself clearly to others. You may talk too much and have a hard time listening to others. You might even eat or drink too much, in a sort of misplaced oral fixation, and you may be prone to dental and gum disease. But when the throat chakra is balanced, you will be able to communicate both your thoughts and your emotions—even emotions like anger and frustration—in a clear, calm, analytical fashion. Your spoken and written words can help you lay the groundwork for healthy relationships and set goals that you can reach.

The throat chakra is blue, so you can use blue crystals there. Try aquamarine, blue lace agate, sodalite, and turquoise.

The sixth chakra, also known as the third eye chakra, is located in the center of your forehead. The sixth chakra is the center of your imagination and your psychic mind. When it is blocked or unbalanced, you might be out of touch with the reality of the physical world. You might seem spacey, or even a little crazy. Alternatively, you might be a little too straight-laced, narrow-minded, or incapable of envisioning any world beyond the rational, linear physical universe. But when the sixth chakra is balanced, you will be able to combine your intuition and your intellect. You will be able to hear—and heed—your sixth sense, and you will be able to use creative visualization to manifest your hopes and dreams.

The sixth chakra is indigo, so you can use indigo crystals there. Try charoite, hawk's eye, lapis lazuli, and sugilite.

The seventh chakra, also known as the crown chakra, is located just above the top of your head. The seventh chakra is your connection to your spirituality, your higher self, and to the divine. It is also the entry point for all of the energy that enters your body and flows down through the rest of your chakras.

The seventh chakra is violet, so you can use violet crystals there. Try amethyst, fluorite, or purple tourmaline.

Because of its association with the spirit, you can also use clear crystals on the seventh chakra, such as clear quartz, danburite, Herkimer diamonds, and selenite.

Pendulums and Chakra Healing

If you have a crystal pendulum on a chain—or a wire-wrapped crystal suspended from a ribbon or a velvet cord—you can use it to move the energy around and through each chakra.

First, make sure you are attuned to your pendulum. Hold the chain, ribbon, or cord between your thumb and index finger so that the pendulum itself dangles about six inches below your hand. Make sure the pendulum is motionless, and then ask it—silently, or with spoken words— to show you which direction it will move for "yes," and which way it will swing for "no."

Once you and your pendulum are synchronized, suspend the pendulum over each chakra, one by one. Ask the pendulum to determine which chakras may need attention.

You can also use your pendulum to balance the chakras. Your intention should be to slow down any chakra that seems to be running in overdrive and to open any chakra that is blocked.

Hold the chain between your thumb and index finger, two or three inches over each chakra. Instead of holding the pendulum still, however, spin it back and forth, clockwise and counterclockwise, by sliding your thumb back and forth. The spinning motion will clear any blockages and help ensure that energy is moving at the right speed.

Healing Grids and Layouts

The chakras are connected through a network of intersecting lines and pathways called meridians, with acupressure points at every intersection. Your entire body, in other words, is a living, breathing, electromagnetic field—a complex grid of chakras, meridian lines, and acupressure points.

You can use that grid as a framework for laying crystals and stones during a healing session. If you know acupressure or acupuncture, you can lay stones on the acupressure points, or use crystal wands or generator points to move energy along the meridian lines.

You can also augment the body's built-in energy system with healing grids based on the patterns of sacred geometry.

Chakra grids and layouts. Choose a simple, chakra-inspired pattern to start. Place a clear crystal above the head, and then work down, laying a color-coded stone on each chakra, a black crystal below the feet, and a clear quartz point in each hand. Then activate the crystals by visualizing a white line of light connecting all of the stones and enabling their energy to circulate freely through your client, in and around his or her own auric field. You can activate the energy with your hands or a wand-shaped crystal.

Don't forget that the chakras run through the entire body, not just the front. People who are getting crystal healing can lay on their stomachs or their backs.

Leave the crystals in place for five or ten minutes, or until they start to roll off. Then remove the crystals, one by one, starting with the hands and feet and moving toward the head.

While the crystals do their work, simply rest quietly and breathe deeply. If you are doing a crystal healing session for another person, remind him or her to relax and breathe deeply, too.

You can devise your own grids, too. You can place them directly on the body, or simply use them in close proximity.

Most healing grids are based on simple geometric patterns, with one power stone in the center and an array of other healing crystals in the rest of the grid. If you like, you can also use quartz points to link the crystals—energy will travel in the direction of their tips or terminations.

Sacred circle. You might want to lay stones in the shape of a sacred circle, the symbol of unity and wholeness.

Spiral magic. You could arrange your crystals in the shape of a spiral to represent the flow of energy through the universe.

Holy trinity. You may want to group your crystals in groups of three, to represent holy trinities like the maiden, mother, and crone, or the father, son, and holy spirit. You can build a triangular-shaped grid of just three crystals, or you can try putting three crystals at the top and bottom of the grid, three in the center, and three on the sides.

Four corners. Try constructing a grid with a healing crystal at all four compass points. You might want each crystal to represent an element, such as earth, air, fire, and water, or a separate area of life, such as the intellectual, the spiritual, the emotional, and the physical. If you plan to lie down in the center of the grid, make sure that you are physically aligned with the cardinal directions—either north and south, or east and west.

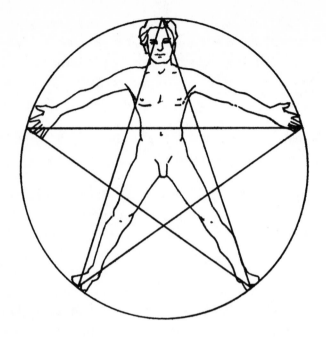

Pentagram. When people stand with their legs apart and their arms outstretched, they form a life-sized pentagram—a star with five points. It's a natural formation for a healing grid. The head is at the top, and the hands and feet complete the pattern. The pentagram is a symbol of all that is good about humanity.

The Star of David is a popular design for healing grids and layouts. The two triangles that make up the star symbolize the union of matter and spirit.

Wheel of the year. You might want to try your hand at a healing grid with eight crystals—one for each eighth of the

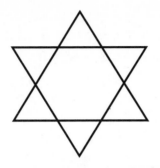

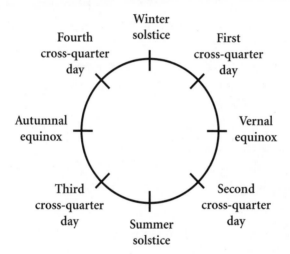

year, based on the seasons and their midpoint cross-quarter days. If you want to add more stones, you could lay twelve—one for each month—or thirteen, for each full moon in a calendar year.

All-purpose grids. You can develop grids for any purpose: prosperity, protection, creativity, or renewal. Simply choose crystals that correspond to your intention.

You can set up grids around your house, in a garden, or inside your home. You can build grids on the ground, or set them up on tables. You can put them under beds or massage tables, or display them on an altar.

You can sketch or print out a grid on a piece of paper, or lay them out by eye.

You can make grids portable by building them in a container. You can use a plate, a ceramic dish, a tile, or a piece of wood. You can even stage crystal grids on top of other, larger crystals. If you want to minimize the movement of the crystals in your grid, fill your base with sand or peat moss first. You might even want to fasten your crystals to an actual grid, like a framework of copper wire.

If you want to construct a complex grid, you might actually be more interested in creating a mandala. Generally speaking, grids are built and left alone to do their work, while mandalas are created as a form of focused, active meditation.

Healing Baths

There is almost nothing as relaxing—and invigorating—as a long, luxurious soak in the tub. Take your crystals into the bath, and you can literally drench yourself in their healing properties.

Stick with hard, quartz-based crystals that won't dissolve or lose their luster in water. Clear quartz, rose quartz, snow quartz, and citrine are ideal.

Run the bath as you normally would. You can add bubbles or relaxing essential oils like lavender and chamomile, or even indulge yourself with a few floating flower petals.

Find yourself a bath pillow or roll up a towel to put under your head. Light candles, dim the lights, and turn on a favorite CD or a meditation tape.

Line your crystals up on the side of the tub so you can bring them into the water after you are already submerged. You don't want to toss them in before you only to step or slip on them as you try to get in. You also don't want to accidentally sit on a crystal and find yourself more imbued with its essence than you had ever intended.

If your crystals and stones are very small and you worry that they could go down the drain, tie them up in a piece of cloth or slip them into a mesh or plastic bag. Their energy and essence will still be able to flow into your bathwater.

Healing Elixirs

Clear crystal elixirs are a fun way to incorporate the healing power of crystals in your everyday life, and making them is remarkable simple.

First, choose a crystal that corresponds to the type of healing you would like to experience—spiritual, emotional, mental, or physical.

Clear quartz will make a good, all-purpose elixir, but you can also make more specialized tonics with colored quartz stones, such as amethyst, carnelian, citrine, rose quartz, and snow quartz.

You might want to avoid using smoky quartz, because its dark color comes about as a result of radiation. In many cases, it occurs naturally and it's completely harmless, but radiation is still something most people don't want to consume, even on a symbolic level.

You should also steer clear of soft crystals that will dissolve or degrade in water. Even if they won't harm you in and of themselves, they could release toxins and bacteria as they dissolve—and your crystals, of course, will be damaged in the process. I recommend varieties of quartz, which are hard.

Do not use artificially colored stones—the dyes could be toxic. And do not make elixirs with metallic stones. Galena, for example, is primarily lead, which no one should consume. Other stones could contain aluminum, arsenic, barium, cadmium, copper, lead, or mercury. Even in trace amounts, such metals could be dangerous.

In other words, don't make elixirs out of any stone or crystal that contains metal. If you don't know the chemical makeup of your crystals, simply avoid green and blue stones because they usually get their color from copper, as well as any stone that looks like it contains metal. If you're not sure if a crystal will be safe to use for an elixir, don't use it.

Once you have chosen a safe crystal for your elixir, clean it, in the literal sense of the word. Use a wet washcloth and a little dish soap. Scrub the crystal and rinse it thoroughly.

As you clean your crystal physically, also cleanse it psychically. Imagine that the soap and water you use are purifying it of any negative energy.

Then put your crystal in a plain glass jar. It really should be very plain: labels, words, designs, or patterns on the jar could imbue your elixir with additional properties, so peel off that pickle label . . . unless you *want* to spice up your spirit with just a hint of baby dill. (However, if you intentionally want to bless your elixir with a specific wish, such as "harmony," "balance," or "wellness," feel free to write the word on the jar, or add a label of your own creation.)

Fill the jar with purified water, spring water, or distilled water, and cover the top of the jar with plastic wrap or a clean piece of cloth.

Put the jar out in the sun for two to four hours, or leave it out overnight in the light of the moon. You might even want to charge your elixir with the power of a particular planet or constellation—simply put it in view of the celestial body of your choice.

Once your elixir has absorbed the power of your crystal, the sun, the moon, or the stars, add an ounce of brandy to stabilize and preserve it. Seal it in a glass container and store it in a cupboard or a refrigerator.

Don't drink the elixir straight: when you're ready to use it, simply add a drop or two to a glass of regular drinking water or juice. You can also add a drop or two to your perfume or cologne.

Healing Plants

You can boost your plants' health, growth, color, and strength by putting crystals in their pots or watering them with crystal elixir. Almost any crystals you feel drawn to intuitively will work—although you should be aware that soft stones like calcite, celestite, lepidolite, and malachite can be damaged by water. Soft stones can also leach into the soil. If they are large or numerous enough, the addition of new minerals into the soil can affect the pH balance and affect plant growth in ways you might not have intended when you planted crystals in the soil.

You can set up crystal sentinels at the entry to your garden, or cairns—pyramid-shaped piles of stones—to serve as focal points for energy.

You could surround your garden with protective crystal guardians, charged with intention to keep deer and rabbits out.

You could even put a decorative medicine wheel or an astrological design in the center of your garden.

Traditionally, green moss agate is said to be the gardener's stone, but all green stones, which symbolize health and growth, are good choices for a garden.

Healing Pets

Crystal healing isn't limited to humans; you can adapt any of the techniques in this book to work with your animal friends. Your dog or cat might lie still while you place crystals on or around his body; you can also wrap crystals with wire and attach them to collars, or sew small stones into their pillows and pet beds.

Distance Healing

If you have another person's permission, you can place crystals around their picture or a map of their location to send healing energy to them from a distance. If you don't have their permission to send healing energy, it could be an invasion of their privacy—and an interference with their personal path. In that case, you could still send your love and good wishes by displaying your crystals with that intent.

Healing Ethics

Before you begin to share your crystal healing techniques with other people, you should be aware that using crystals to heal other people will put you in a position of power— power that you must be determined to use wisely and well.

Your primary objective should be to remember the advice of Hippocrates, the ancient Greek physician who said, "First, do no harm."

Ethically, healing can be a slippery slope. Unless you are a trained medical professional, you should never represent yourself as a expert health care practitioner or advisor—for your own legal protection, as well as the life, safety, and well-being of those you try to help. Be sure that you don't present yourself as something that you're not, or make crystals out to be a magic solution to all of a person's ills—literally or figuratively.

Be especially aware that your role as a healer, even if you are just experimenting with various techniques, is a powerful one. Realize that when you pull out your crystals, whatever you say could seem to be coming from some higher source, and the words you use will carry a much greater weight than they would under normal circumstances. Don't make any promises you can't keep, and don't say anything that could be misinterpreted. Be especially careful not

to make any self-fulfilling prophecies. Don't ever predict—
or even hint at—death, sickness, injury, or doom. Instead,
put all of your comments and suggestions in the best possible light.

Mystical Crystals

An Alphabetical Guide to
Crystals, Rocks, and Stones

It wasn't easy to choose just a few crystals for the "Top Twenty" recommendations in this guide. There are hundreds of crystals on today's market—and there are thousands of types of combination crystals, too.

Once you start collecting, don't limit yourself to following any strict guidelines. Shop around, buy what you like, and feel free to add any stone that catches your eye. You can even use this list as a starting point for all the crystals you would like to own ... someday.

Here is an alphabetical guide to common crystals, rocks, and stones.

Abalone is not technically a crystal. It's a flat, open shell with a mother-of-pearl sheen inside. Sometimes known as sea ears, many people like to use abalone shells to burn incense (on a layer of sand) for use during cleansing and smudging rituals.

Agates come in a wide variety of colors and appearances. They are good crystals to use when you need a little help with logical thinking.

- **Blue lace agates** feature cascading bands of blue and white, reminiscent of sea and sky. Use them when you want to contemplate the depths of emotion or of higher consciousness.

- **Botswana agates**, with their smoky-colored rings, are strongly recommended for firefighters, as well as people who smoke, those who want to quit smoking, and those who come into regular contact with excessive amounts of heat or smoke.

- **Dendritic agates** are associated with agriculture and plant life, and related concepts like growth, plenitude, and the abundance of nature. Gaze into a dendritic agate, and you will see the silhouetted outline of trees and forests. Tuck dendritic agates next to your houseplants to give them a boost.

- **Fern agates**—in which each striation seems to be a miniature, leafy fern—help us communicate with plants and attune us to the world of devas and nature spirits.

- **Fire agates**, filled with opalescent, lavalike swirls, can help you feel more courageous, assertive, and enthusiastic. Use fire agate to add spark to your writing.

- **Moss agates**, with their deep, mossy-green color, are sometimes called the gardener's stone because they can help you grow plants and wealth.

- **Tree agates**, with their leafy green striations, seem to display images of leafy boughs. Climb the branches of a tree agate to new heights of consciousness, or take one into your backyard to get an overview of your home life.

Alexandrite, which changes from green in daylight to red in incandescent light, was discovered in Russia in 1830. It was named after Czar Alexander II, whose imperial colors were red and green. Use alexandrite when you want to experience a dramatic transformation, see yourself in a new light, or get in touch with your own regal nature.

Amazonite, a green form of feldspar, can help you unlock your Amazon warrior spirit. It is especially good at helping you find your voice and develop your communication skills. It is even said to have healing properties for the throat and lungs, which is one reason musicians have traditionally used it. Some gamblers carry amazonite for luck.

Amber, which is petrified sap from a prehistoric pine tree, can help you discover ancient wisdom and knowledge. Some amber stones even contain the preserved bodies of prehistoric insects. Amber has been popular for thousands of years, as an elixir, in jewelry and amulets, and as a talisman. It's one of the few stones that can be electrically charged, which means it can generate heat quickly and efficiently.

Amethyst—see the "Starter Sets" chapter.

Ametrine, a combination of amethyst and citrine, combines the yellow energizing power of the sun with the spiritual properties of amethyst in a single bicolored gemstone. Ametrine is a good stone to use when you want to utilize your full range of talents, or when you want to join forces with another person or group.

Andalusite—see chiastolite and fairy cross.

Angel aura—see rainbow aura.

Angelite, a beautiful sky-blue stone, is used to connect with angels, spirit guides, and the higher self. It can also help you with telepathy, psychic awareness, astral travel, and lucid dreaming.

Apache tears take their name from a legend about a group of Apache Indians who were ambushed by an enemy tribe, driven to the top of a high bluff, and forced to leap to their deaths. Their grief-stricken wives wept over the bodies, and their tears became the translucent black obsidian stones we know today. According to the legend, whoever owns Apache tears will never cry again because enough tears have already been shed.

Apatite, whose name comes from the Greek word for "deceive" because it is often mistaken for other minerals, comes in a wide range of colors and shapes: white, brown, yellow, green, blue, purple, and red. Apatite can help you alter your appearance, too—especially if you want to lose weight.

Aqua aura is clear quartz dipped in molten gold, so it has a light, metallic-blue tint and built-in shielding abilities.

Aquamarine, the favorite stone of sailors, is attuned to the ocean and spirit of the sea and all the associated properties of water. During the Middle Ages, it was said that people who held an aquamarine in their mouths could call the devil from hell and force him to answer their questions. Aquamarines are also supposed to guarantee happiness, wealth, and a happy marriage.

Aragonite, a form of calcite, usually comes in a cluster that looks like it took form in a sudden burst of energy. Aragonite can add a burst of energy to your projects and personality, too.

Aventurine—see the "Starter Sets" chapter.

Azurite is good for psychic work, and it's an integral part of many crystal and gemstone-healing layouts. Its deep, cobalt-blue color will help you go deep within yourself for psychological and spiritual insights. During the Middle Ages and the Renaissance, European painters loved azurite for the beautiful blue pigment it lent to their art.

Barite, a sky-blue stone, is favored by many Native Americans, who use it to transform from physical to spiritual beings in their ceremonial practices. Barite is also said to inspire lucid dreams and dream recall.

Basalt stones, formed when volcanic lava cools and hardens, are dark and smooth. Basalt stones hold heat consistently and are ideal for hot stone massage.

Beryls are colorless, at least in their pure form. In fact, it's actually their impurities that make most beryls so valuable. Emeralds, for example, are beryls, as are aquamarines. Other types of beryls include golden beryl, which is also known as heliodor, a powerful reminder of the sun's light and energy. Pink beryls, also known as morganite, can soothe raw emotions and stimulate healing, and red beryl, also known as bixbite, is a vibrant, purplish-red stone that can bring new life to longstanding relationships and stimulate the circulatory system.

Biotite—see mica.

Bixbite—see beryl.

Bloodstone—see the "Starter Sets" chapter.

Blue tiger's eye—see hawk's eye.

Boji Stones are magnetic stones with a high concentration of iron. Boji Stones are usually sold in sets—one rough "male" stone, and one smooth "female" stone that work together to demonstrate the give and take of daily life. They can help you balance the feminine and masculine aspects of your personality, or smooth wide-ranging emotions and experiences. (The name "Boji Stones" is a trademark of Boji, Inc. They are also called Kansas Pop Rocks.)

Bornite—see peacock ore.

Brazilianite, a greenish-yellow crystal discovered in Brazil in 1945, is heavier than it looks. Because people are still learning about its properties, Brazilianite is associated with academic achievement, attention to detail, study skills, and intelligence.

Bustamite, which ranges in color from pale pink to reddish brown, can "bust through" energy blockages and, like all red stones, it can help with love and health issues.

Calcite, which gets its name from the Greek word for "lime," is one of the most common minerals on earth—it comprises about 4 percent of the earth's crust. Despite the fact that calcite is everywhere, collectors value it for its beauty and variations. Calcite is also known as Iceland spar, lime spar, pineapple jasper, Mexican jade, and Mexican onyx.

Carnelian—see the "Starter Sets" chapter.

Cat's eye, a form of chrysoberyl, is often confused with tiger's eye, but it's rarer. Cat's eye has a distinct band of light across its face which sweeps from side to side. Just as cats can see in the dark, you can use cat's eye crystals to peer into areas that could use some illumination.

Celestite, with its impressionistic points of white and blue, certainly reflects a celestial theme. Some people believe that it can connect us to guardian and guiding angels. It can also help those who would like to try astral travel.

Chalcedony is a catchall term for translucent quartz. The chalcedony family includes agates, aventurine, bloodstone, carnelians, chrysoprase, flint, jasper, and onyx.

Charoite was discovered in 1947 near the Chara River in Siberia, where Russia's political prisoners were often exiled. Because of this, the crystal has come to be seen as an aid to those who feel—or fear—exile from others. Charoite wasn't introduced to the West until 1978.

Chevron amethysts, with their distinctive V-shaped markings, combine the clarifying qualities of clear quartz with the royal qualities of purple amethyst.

Chiastolite, also known as cross stone, fairy cross, andalusite, chiastolite, and staurolite, is a variety of andalusite. When it is sliced, you can clearly see a cross shape in the stone. As a result, it can symbolize Christianity, devotion, death, rebirth, and immortality.

Chinese writing stone, which originates in the Yangtze River Valley in China, seems to be inscribed with characters from the Chinese alphabet. Use it when you want to improve your writing and communication skills. Some believe it can also help us access the Akashic Record, the cosmic repository of all knowledge.

Chrysoberyl—see cat's eye.

Chrysocolla, also known as gem silica, features distinctive rings of blue and green—which almost look like contour maps of dark blue islands, floating on a turquoise sea. Use chrysocolla when you want to explore uncharted territory, or develop a map of your own consciousness.

Chrysoprase, with its distinctive green-apple hue, hearkens back to the original forbidden fruit in the Garden of Eden. Chrysoprase is frequently used to renew love and passion between long-married couples. Don't leave it in direct sunlight, however, or its color will fade.

Chrysotile is asbestos, which can be quite dangerous to one's health. If you own a mineral sample of chrysotile, do not cut it, drill it, sand it, break it, or flake it. Don't confuse chrysotile with the harmless crystal chrysolite, an off-green variety of peridot.

Citrine—see the "Starter Sets" chapter.

Coral is treasured by crystal collectors, even though it's not a crystal. In ancient times, coral branches were cast as a fortune-telling device. Little girls wore coral necklaces for luck, and travelers carried coral for protection whenever they had to voyage by sea. Because coral is a form of sea life that grows in large communities, you can refer to it when you need help living and working with other people.

Danburite, a clear crystal that sometimes has a subtle pink hue, was originally found in the area around Danbury, Connecticut. Because Danburite is remarkably clear and brilliant, it can be a useful tool when you need to think clearly and come up with brilliant new ideas.

Desert rose crystals, formed of sand and light brown gypsum, bloom from the mineral-rich groundwater beneath the surface of deserts in Mexico and Morocco. They are a form of selenite. While desert roses are extremely fragile, they are also exquisitely beautiful. They are fun to hold in the open palm of your hand, especially when you want to contemplate areas of your life in which you can blossom and grow. They can serve as a gentle reminder that surprising creations can spring from an area that looks dry and deserted at first glance.

Diamond, the hardest mineral, has long been a symbol of perfection, durability, and endless love. Diamonds also symbolize brilliance and material success. Some people believe that diamonds amplify the properties of other crystals.

Diopside, which is usually green, also comes in brown and white, as well as a rare blue variety called violan. The most interesting variety is star diopside, which features a four-rayed star that might make you think of Venus, the morning and evening star.

Dioptase crystals come in shades of radiant, rich green. They actually look like scale models of the Emerald City, straight from *The Wizard of Oz*. Use dioptase when you want to fantasize about starting a new life or when you wonder if the grass really is greener on the other side.

Dolomite is an interesting crystal because scientists can't quite explain how it is formed. Apparently, dolomite starts its existence as a form of limestone, but somehow, in a process just short of metamorphosis, the calcite and aragonite it contains are transformed into dolomite. For that reason, you might want to have dolomite on hand if you are dealing with issues of dramatic transformation, but you don't want to become a completely different person.

Dumortierite, a form of blue quartz that can come in shades of deep violet, is a popular ornamental stone. It is often carved into beads, eggs, spheres, and cabochons.

Emeralds have been treasured throughout history. Their characteristic green color is not only breathtaking, but it also symbolizes life, growth, fertility, and creativity. The ancient Incas and Aztecs in South America believed emeralds were holy. Gemstone mines near the Red Sea were favored by Egyptian pharaohs between 3000 and 1500 BC. The Vedas, the ancient sacred writings of Hinduism, say that emeralds are lucky stones that enhance well-being.

Epidote, which usually comes in shades of green, is a stone of increase and growth.

Fairy cross (or fairy stone) comes in the shape of a cross. In addition to its obvious link to Christianity, the stone is also said to represent the four elements of earth, air, fire, and water. Fairy cross makes a natural good luck charm. It is sometimes called andalusite, chiastolite, or staurolite.

Flint, a gray, white, black, red, or brown variety of quartz found all around the world, was one of the first stones used as a tool. Prehistoric workers crafted flint into knives, scrapers, arrows, and pipes. With its highly polished sheen and attractive color variations, flint still makes a good tool for meditation.

Fluorite—see the "Starter Sets" chapter.

Fool's gold—see pyrite.

Fossils connect us to the past, both on a personal level and in a cosmic sense. Because fossils are literally the bones of the past, they are associated with the skeletal system, bones, hands, and feet.

Fulgurite is solidified lightning—or technically, it's sand, melted and fused by lightning strikes on the beach. Most fulgurite crystals are shaped like long, hollow tubes, and they look like small twigs and branches. You can use fulgurite when you need a flash of inspiration, or when you wouldn't mind a bolt from the blue.

Fuchsite, like all green crystals, can stimulate growth, financial success, creativity, and healing.

Gaia stone is green obsidian from the volcanic ash of Mt. St. Helens. Gaia was the mythological Mother Earth goddess who originated at the time of creation and gave birth to all life. Many people associate Gaia stone with the earth and goddess archetypes.

Galaxite, also known as galaxyite, is a granular black stone. Galaxite is sometimes called the aura stone because energy healers use it to cleanse, balance, and protect the aura.

Galena is lead, which can be toxic, so it should be handled with care. It is mesmerizing and beautiful, however, and its shiny surfaces can inspire reflection.

Garnet, traditionally worn to attract lovers, symbolizes devotion and long-term commitment. Occasionally, good friends exchange it to ensure that they will meet again. Garnets range in color from deep emerald green through yellow, brown, and red. Garnets have always been thought of as protective stones because people thought they were bright enough to light a path through darkness. In fact, according to one legend, Noah used a garnet lantern to light the ark.

Gem silica—see chrysocolla.

Goldstone was originally created by alchemists who were trying to make gold. It is glass with glittery metallic material in it. Even though it is man-made, it is still a beautiful stone and is both fascinating and uplifting to look at. Blue goldstone can be used to remind us of the beauty of the night sky, and it helps us remember that light can be found even in darkness.

Goshenite, a clear, colorless beryl, was used to make eyeglasses in ancient times. Even today, contemplating a goshenite crystal can help you focus, filter out distractions, and visualize the location of a lost object.

Granite is a common rock that comes in shades of gray, white, pink, and green. Because it is a composite of many smaller crystals (primarily quartz and feldspar), granite can be used to represent community issues—and because it is often used as a building material, it can also be used as a token of relationship building.

Grossularite is a type of garnet. It comes out of the earth lumpy, bumpy, and rather misshapen looking, but it polishes beautifully.

Gypsum is a sedimentary rock that often forms in massive beds as saltwater evaporates, so you can associate it with the sea, the sun, and the sand. It is usually gray or white.

Halite, which is actually rock salt, is usually pink or white. Because it is literally the salt of the earth, it is good for grounding, cleansing, and protection.

Hawk's eye, also known as blue tiger's eye, is quartz, usually in shades of blue-green to blue-gray. Use it when you need a clear overview of a situation or when you are hunting for answers.

Heliodor is a golden form of beryl, named after Helios, the Greek god of the sun. Each morning, Helios rose at dawn and traveled the sky in a chariot pulled by four golden horses. Use heliodor when you want to travel—spiritually, at least—from one horizon to another.

Heliotrope—see bloodstone in the "Starter Sets" chapter.

Hematite—see the "Starter Sets" chapter.

Herkimer diamonds were found originally in Herkimer, New York. They look a lot like diamonds, but they're actually quartz. Many are double terminated, and it's not unusual to find Herkimer diamonds with enhydros, which are bubbles of trapped air and water. Some people use Herkimer diamonds to enhance their dreams, boost astral travel, or recall past lives.

Hiddenite is a green stone, and it is best known for attracting prosperity.

Howlite—see the "Starter Sets" chapter.

Iceland spar—see calcite.

Indicolite—a blue form of tourmaline.

Infinite, a blend of serpentine and chrysotile from South Africa, has come to be known as the healer's stone because it reportedly pulls pain out of the body. Some healers believe that it works on a cellular level to disperse crystallized energy.

Iolite was treasured by Viking navigators, who found they could use it as a filter to look directly at the sun without damaging their eyes. The stone is normally a deep violet-blue, but it has pleochroic properties, meaning that it can also look clear or yellow, depending on how it is cut. Take iolite with you when you travel, use it as a navigational aid in your spiritual journeys, or keep it as a touchstone for any venture into unexplored territory. While you probably don't want to use it to look at the sun, some people believe that iolite can facilitate psychic visions.

Jade comes in two varieties: jadeite and a creamier, less translucent nephrite. Jade is usually green, but it can also come in blue, black, violet, white, yellow, red, and brown. Because jade is remarkably durable—stronger than steel, in fact—it has become known as the stone of longevity. In China, jade has been treasured since at least 2950 BC. The ancient Chinese believed that jade could preserve the body after death; one tomb contained an entire suit made out of jade to assure the physical immortality of its owner. In Central America, the Olmecs, the Mayans, and the Toltecs all treasured jade and used it for carvings and masks.

Jasper—see the "Starter Sets" chapter.

Jet, a black form of petrified wood similar to coal, can help you through the darkness of depression or serve as a guide through the dark, hidden mysteries of psychic experience.

Kansas pop rocks—see Boji Stones.

Kunzite is the pink variety of spodumene. Because it is pink, kunzite is associated with gentleness, friendliness, emotional balance, and compassion.

Kyanite, which comes in shades of green, blue, and black, is a layered stone that can help you peel back the layers of your personality or even uncover past life experiences. Kyanite is also a good stone for channeling.

Labradorite, also called spectrolite, might seem like a dull, ordinary dark rock at first. In the right light, however—and once it has been polished and cut—labradorite becomes one of the world's most fascinating, beautiful minerals, with a rainbow-colored sheen that seems to dance across its surface. Labradorite serves as a tangible reminder that people, too, hold gifts and talents that should not be overlooked.

Lapis lazuli—see the "Starter Sets" chapter.

Larimar is as blue as the Caribbean Sea—which, coincidentally, is the only place it can be found, in the Dominican Republic. Gazing at larimar is as soothing as watching waves roll over a white, sandy beach. Larimar is sometimes known as Atlantis stone or dolphin stone.

Lavulite—see sugilite.

Lead—see galena.

Lepidolite, a lovely lavender stone, contains both mica and lithium. Lithium is often prescribed in pharmaceutical form to people who suffer from bipolar disorder or severe depression. Likewise, lepidolite is a stone for people who need to balance their moods and calm negative emotions, anxiety, or addictions, or to sleep better. Lepidolite is fragile, and it should not be soaked in water.

Lemurian seed crystals are wand-shaped crystals. They usually have a lot of broken edges, and they are covered with distinct, deeply etched ridges. Those markings play a key role in a rich and complex legend that surrounds the crystals. According to the story, Lemurian seed crystals were all encoded with the knowledge and history of an ancient civilization in the Pleiades star system. The crystals were planted—or seeded—on Earth to attract Pleiadian souls to reincarnated lives on this planet, and to unite our civilizations across time and space.

Lodestone, a furry-looking magnetic stone, has been used for thousands of years in amulets and talismans. It is a tangible reminder of the power of attraction, reportedly able to draw power, good fortune, and love to anyone who holds it.

Luvulite—see sugilite.

Magnesite doesn't usually form crystals on its own, but it is a major component of a wide variety of other stones, such as aragonite, dolomite, and serpentine. It is, for the most part, calcite, so it is associated with bones and teeth. Magnesite is usually white or gray.

Magnetite, a black iron ore, is naturally magnetic, so it can be used to attract love, luck, and health. Magnetite is a form of hematite.

Malachite—see the "Starter Sets" chapter.

Marble, smooth and cold to the touch, has always been a favorite material of artists and craftsmen. Michelangelo envisioned greatness in the powerful stone. Use marble when you want to free the god or goddess within yourself.

Marcasite, also called white pyrite, is a silvery form of iron. Because of its high iron content, it is sometimes used as an aid to help women recover from childbirth, when their blood is frequently depleted of iron.

Meteorites like tektite and moldavite prove that it is possible to catch a falling star. Most meteorites are dark brown or black, and pitted and mottled from their descent through our atmosphere. Meteorites symbolize travel across great distances, lifelong journeys, and long-distance communication. You can use a meteorite when you want to connect to other worlds or tune in to the energy of the universe.

Micas are a group of minerals found in all types of rocks—igneous, metamorphic, and sedimentary. The three most common mica minerals are muscovite, biotite, and lepidolite. While mica flakes are brittle, mica crystals can withstand high temperatures and environments that erode other minerals. Use mica when you want to persevere through a pressure-filled situation.

Mirror apophyllite is a favorite crystal among collectors, who are drawn to its shape; most apophyllite ends in a four-sided pyramid or a straight-edged cube formation. Usually colorless or white, apophyllite also comes in shades of pastel green. Because apophyllite is so shiny, many people believe it has the power to reflect the past and reveal the truth.

Mochi marbles, also known as moki balls, moqui marbles, or shaman stones, were named after a Native American tribe in the Moqui Desert, who used the balls to play games. Mochi balls contain iron and sandstone, and they usually are sold in pairs—a rough "male" ball and a smooth "female" sphere. They often have a slight magnetic charge, which further reinforces their association with attraction, partnerships, and duality.

Moldavite, a misty green meteoric stone, is a rare variety of tektite.

Moonstone—see the "Starter Sets" chapter.

Morganite, or pink beryl, was named in honor of banker J. P. Morgan. Like emeralds and aquamarines, morganite is a beryl.

Morion is a naturally dark crystal, blackened from exposure to natural radiation. Use morion if you want to explore shadow issues—such as "negative" thoughts and feelings—or contemplate the hidden aspects of your unconscious.

Mother-of-pearl is another organic substance that frequently finds its way into crystal collections. It isn't a stone; rather, it is the opalescent, pearly lining of an oyster shell. Mother-of-pearl is usually associated with protection as well as the calming, peaceful nature of the ocean.

Muscovite, a form of mica, is found both in crystal form and in layered sheets. Muscovite can form an insulating barrier against heat; in fact, oven windows used to be made of muscovite. You might want to use muscovite when you want a layer of protection between yourself and a particularly hot issue.

Nebula stone is black with nebula-like markings for access to cosmic wisdom and understanding.

Nephrite is a creamier, less translucent form of jade.

Novaculite is a form of white quartz commonly used to make whetstones for sharpening knives, razors, and other steel implements. In metaphysical circles, novaculite is also known as the cord-cutting crystal. Some healers use it to cut psychic or etheric cords; it can also be used to cut through clutter, cut straight to the heart of an issue, and cut through problems.

Obsidian—see the "Starter Sets" chapter.

Okenite is a white mineral that looks a lot like cotton balls. It's sometimes called "a warm and fuzzy" stone because it inspires warm, fuzzy feelings of comfort and acceptance.

Olivine—see peridot in "Starter Sets."

Onyx is usually black or brown, and sometimes it has bands of white and tan. It's easy to imagine stories based on the shapes or patterns in its markings. Black onyx owes its rich, solid color to an ancient dying process that is still in use today. According to legend, onyx has been known to cool the fires of passion, and even provoke discord and arguments between lovers.

Opals reflect a wide variety of colors—they put on a constant, glittering show of flashing lights, like lightning on a smaller scale, or the sun breaking through clouds as it rises or sets. Opal is fragile, and it can crack if it is left in direct sunlight or if it gets too hot. Even under normal conditions, it should be moistened frequently with water or oil. The Romans believed opal was the symbol of hope and purity, and they thought it could keep wearers safe from disease. The ancient Greeks thought opal was a prophetic stone. In the Middle Ages, opal was prescribed for poor eyesight, blonde women wore opal necklaces to keep their hair color bright and pure, and thieves carried opal because they thought it would make them invisible. Opal might be able to help you be inconspicuous in situations where you don't care to be noticed.

Orange millennium, a newly discovered form of carnelian, is found only in the high desert of the U.S. Southwest. The distinctive round nodules are said to be good for detoxification of both the mind and the body.

Orthoclase—see moonstone in "Starter Sets."

Peacock ore, the stone of happiness, is a bright blue form of bornite with a multicolored sheen. It's a reminder that sometimes it's okay for you to strut like a peacock. Use it when you feel especially proud of an accomplishment or when you want to show off a bit.

Pearls are formed in response to irritation—they start as a single grain of sand that gets covered with layer after layer of a gleaming, lustrous, jewel-like nacre. Pearls, in other words, symbolize a perfection that has its foundation in hardship. The growth of a pearl is a metaphor for human development—we, too, have the power to transform pain and to gain wisdom from difficult situations. Pearls are connected to both the sea and the moon, just as the moon has the power to affect the tidal waves of emotion. You can use a pearl when you want to better attune yourself to the ebb and flow of life.

Pearl aura—see rainbow aura.

Peridot—see the "Starter Sets" chapter.

Petalite is sometimes called the stone of the angels because its light pink color suggests a link to the higher realms.

Petrified wood—see the "Starter Sets" chapter.

Phenakite takes its name from the Greek word that means imposter because it can look deceptively similar to quartz.

Picasso marble, also known as Picasso stone and Picasso jasper, looks like Picasso himself painted each stone in his distinctive cubist style. For that reason, it's sometimes referred to as the artist's stone. Use it to free your creativity.

Pink manganocalcite, or pink magnesium calcite, is sometimes called the Reiki stone. Healers like it because it seems to magnify their own healing energies and efforts.

Prehnite, the yellowish-green stone of remembered dreams, is sometimes recommended as a crystal for lucid dreaming, dream recall, meditation, and prophecy.

Purpurite, named for its distinctive purple color, would be a regal stone for anyone in a position of leadership and authority—especially if that role involves a spiritual component.

Pyrite, commonly known as fool's gold, is anything but foolish. Pyrite is associated with intelligence, logic, and clear thinking. Pyrite has been used for ornamental pieces and in jewelry for thousands of years. In South America, Incans created scrying mirrors from large slabs of polished pyrite. According to legend, the ancient Chinese earth symbol, a golden cube, was derived from pyrite.

Pyromorphite, the victory stone, often looks like a cartoon cactus, because it is green with little bumps and "needles" all over.

Quantum-quattro silica is a combination of minerals found only in Namibia—chrysocolla, shattuckite, malachite, dioptase, and smoky quartz.

Quartz is the mainstay of the crystal world. It is a versatile, multipurpose stone. Quartz crystals can grow singularly or in groups, and they come in all shapes, sizes, and colors. Most quartz crystals are six-sided.

Well-known stones like agate, amethyst, carnelian, chalcedony, jasper, onyx, and tiger's eye are all forms of quartz.

- **Blue quartz**, which comes in shades of blue, gray, and lavender, is a fairly rare stone, found in the United States and Brazil. Like all blue-colored stones, blue quartz is calming, peaceful, and serene.

- **Chalcedony quartz** is not a single crystal, but a collection of finely grained microcrystals. Chalcedony quartz is even more varied than clear quartz, because it can come in any color or pattern. Agates, carnelian, jasper, onyx, and tiger's eye are all members of the chalcedony family.

- **Clear quartz**, a transparent, colorless crystal also known as rock crystal, may be the most popular stone of all. Mystics have loved clear quartz for centuries. They believe it can purify the air, cleanse and clear the environment, amplify thoughts and feelings, clarify one's thinking, and speed spiritual development and healing. Pure white light passes through it easily.

- **Dendritic quartz** tells its story through markings that look like the branches of a tree. "Dendritic," in fact, means branched, like a tree.

- **Drusy quartz** is covered with other tiny sparking crystals, and each one will catch and reflect light on its own.

- **Milky quartz**, also called snow quartz, is white and cloudy, like milk. Sometimes, inclusions of milky quartz are responsible for the ghostly phantom crystals in clear quartz. Milky quartz is calming and relaxing, and it makes a good gift for children.

- **Purple quartz** should not be confused with amethyst. It has a dark violet color and may have inclusions or clouding within it.

- **Rose quartz** is the stone of peace and emotional healing. It's also a romantic stone—its rosy color is associated with all forms of love and friendship.

- **Rutilated quartz** is clear quartz with metallic gold, copper, or blue-gray titanium inclusions, which are sometimes called Venus hair. The fibers are fascinating to look at, and they add new depths and direction to any energy that passes through the stone.

- **Smoky quartz** is translucent brown, black, or smoky gray. Some people believe that it can filter and trap the negative thoughts and emotions of other people, while others suggest that it can actually send negativity back to its source and prompt the person to rethink his or her attitude. Carrying a smoky quartz can help you be more selective in the type of people you choose to be around.

- **Snow quartz**—see milky quartz.

- **Spirit quartz**, also known as porcupine quartz, cactus quartz, and spirit crystal, is covered with smaller crystals pointing in all directions. Like all crystals that feature multiple groupings, you can use spirit quartz when you want to work with large groups of people or if you want to direct your energy into multiple fields.

- **Tourmalated quartz** is clear or milky quartz blended with needlelike strands of black tourmaline. The blend of light and darkness might prompt you to think about the contrasts and contradictions you carry within yourself—your light side and your shadow, your conscious and your unconscious mind, your masculine and feminine sides of your personality. Tourmalated quartz is a powerful stone to use when you are dealing with dualities and polarities of any kind, and it can help you find harmony even in opposition.

Rainbow aura, also known as angel aura, opal aura, and pearl aura, is quartz that has been infused with platinum. Technicians put the stone in a 1,600-degree vacuum filled with chemically purified platinum vapors. The platinum is permanently bonded to the surface of the crystal, which results in a breathtaking, opalescent sheen. The rainbow colors of a rainbow aura can remind you of the clearing skies after a rainstorm and brighter days to come.

Rainforest rhyolite is a form of jasper.

Rhodochrosite means rose-colored, and in fact, its vivid hue is remarkable. Some call rhodochrosite the stone of love and balance. Its variegated, rosy hues can remind you to enjoy love and romance, all in the proper balance.

Rhodonite—see the "Starter Sets" chapter.

Rhodozite crystals are tiny, ten-sided crystals from Madagascar. Extremely rare, rhodozite is said to enhance any crystal it comes near and never need cleaning.

Riverstones are smooth, rounded pebbles found in rivers and on beaches. They become naturally polished as water and other rocks move against them.

Rubellite is pink to red tourmaline.

Ruby. For thousands of years, ruby has been considered one of the most valuable gemstones of our earth. Ruby is a corundum, which is colorless in its pure form. Add a hint of chrome, iron, titanium, or vanadium, however, and you'll get a ruby—or a sapphire. Some rubies feature a starry flash of light in their center, which is known as asterism. The intense red of a ruby symbolizes power, passion, and desire.

Sapphire, the stone of prosperity, is also a corundum, which makes it the sister of the ruby. Ancient Persians believed that the sky was a gigantic blue sapphire stone. It's true that sapphires come in all shades of blue, from the cerulean blue of a summer sky to the deep blue of twilight. Sapphire also comes in related sunset colors of orange, pink, purple, and yellow.

Sard is porous, reddish-brown quartz.

Sardonyx, a form of onyx, features layers of sard and onyx in bands of red, brown, black, and white. Sardonyx was highly valued in Rome, especially for seals, because it was said to never stick to the wax. Roman general Publius Cornelius Scipio was known for wearing lots of sardonyx.

Satin spar—see selenite.

Selenite, a clear, striated gypsum, was named after Selene, Greek goddess of the moon. Selenite, also known as satin spar, comes as a shimmering clear crystal and in a form called a rosette. Alabaster, an ornamental stone used in fine carvings for centuries, is also a form of selenite. Use selenite if you are dealing with issues that seem to come and go on a regular basis like the moon. Because Selene was said to be the mother of fifty children, you can also use selenite if you are pregnant, trying to get pregnant, raising children, or dealing with your own mother.

Seraphinite, a vivid green crystal, is often referred to as an angel stone. In the traditional medieval hierarchy of angels, a seraph held the highest rank. Use a seraphinite crystal to contact or thank your guardian angel.

Serpentine comes in various shades of green. Some people believe it can guard against the bites and stings of venomous creatures. On a metaphysical level, it is also thought to help with the rise of kundalini, or "serpent fire" energy through the chakras.

Shaman stones—see mochi marbles.

Shiva lingam stones are found only near the Narmada River, one of India's seven holy sites. During the dry season, the stones are collected from the riverbed. Shiva lingam stones are fertility stones; *lingam* is Sanskrit for phallus, and the stones symbolize the Hindu god, Lord Shiva, himself. The markings on a shiva lingam stone, however, symbolize yoni or female energy, for the perfect balance of masculine and feminine.

Silica is the highest, purest form of gem-quality chrysocolla.

Smithsonite, also known as bonamite, usually comes in grapelike clusters of light green, blue-green, lavender, and purple. It was named after James Smithson, the founder of the Smithsonian Institution. Smithsonite is a gorgeous crystal, and like other stones that form in clusters and groups, it can help you with your relationships and community endeavors.

Snowflake obsidian is black obsidian.

Sodalite—see the "Starter Sets" chapter.

Spectrolite—see labradorite.

Spinel crystals come in a variety of reds, greens, and blues. Historically used as a substitute for rubies and other gemstones, spinel is most often put to metaphysical work as a detoxifier.

Staurolite—see chiastolite and fairy cross.

Stichtite, a rosy, purple-colored crystal, is formed when continental plates collide. In the home, where personalities can also collide, stichtite can help create a tranquil, quake-free environment—especially if children and immature adults in that home happen to be prone to emotional outbursts.

Sugilite, also known as luvulite (or lavulite) and royal azel, is sometimes known as the healer's stone. It comes in varying shades of pink, purple, and violet. It is frequently used by healers to draw pain from the body—or the psyche—and instill peace of mind.

Sulfur, a vivid yellow mineral that almost looks chemically enhanced, hints at both physical and metaphysical brightness. Because yellow is often associated with sunlight and air, sulfur is said to clear and enlighten the mind.

Sunstone, also called aventurine, feldspar, or oligoclase, can help you dispel clouds of negativity and fear, radiate health, happiness, and good fortune, and assume your natural place as a leader and center of attention.

Tanzanite, a blue form of zoisite, is sometimes called the workaholic's stone. Masai herdsmen discovered it in Tanzania in 1967, and Tiffany's jewelers introduced the stone to the public two years later. Its color ranges from ultramarine to a light, purplish blue, making it an ideal crystal for relaxation and dreamwork.

Tektite is a type of meteoric glass, found only in Australia, the Philippines, Thailand, and Vietnam. Like other meteors, they are generally pitted, and some seem to have been stretched in a molten state. While tektites were originally thought to have fallen from outer space, scientists now tend to think that tektites are actually earth rocks that melted when meteorites fell on them.

Thulite, which is sometimes called unionite, is a red form of zoisite.

Tiger iron helps with creative endeavors and all types of artistic abilities.

Tiger's eye—see the "Starter Sets" chapter.

Topaz was once thought to be tinted with the golden glow of the Egyptian sun god Ra. The ancient Greeks believed that topaz could make people stronger—and even invisible.

Tourmaline, a breathtaking, rainbow-colored stone, has been used for more than 2,000 years. In medieval times, tourmaline was thought to heal the sick and even prevent death. Tourmaline stones show a wide range of colors, depending on how you look at them. Some specimens also feature a cat's-eye chatoyancy. Tourmaline comes in many colors: black, blue, brown, green, opalized, pink, red, and watermelon.

Turquoise has been a holy stone, good luck charm, and talisman for thousands of years. Its famous color is the result of two components: blue from copper, and green from iron or chromium. Its color will actually change, sometimes, depending on the body chemistry of the person who wears it or holds it. The ancient Egyptians included turquoise with the bodies of its pharaohs in the tombs, and Persians wore turquoise to ward off the evil eye. The Aztecs in Northern Peru used turquoise to decorate their ceremonial masks, and some Native Americans believed that turquoise was a link between lake and sky.

Turquonite is howlite that has been dyed blue to resemble turquoise. It is often falsely sold as turquoise.

Ulexite, also known as lexite, is a desert stone formed in alkali salt flats. Ulexite is commonly known as the "TV stone." If you set a ulexite slab on a piece of paper with writing, the words seem to be projected onto the crystal. However, if you look at a slab of ulexite from the side, the stone looks completely opaque. Ulexite is a good stone to use if you want to project a message to the outside world or get insight into yourself or other people. Ulexite is a soft stone, and it could fall apart if you soak it in water.

Unakite, which is sometimes spelled unikite, is pink and green—or more specifically, coral and olive. It consists of three minerals: feldspar, epidote, and quartz. Some people believe that unakite is a good stone for pregnant women to carry, and that it can boost the health of both mother and child.

Variscite is a cool, pale green stone that looks a lot like turquoise. It can help you cool down when you feel overwhelmed by worry, tension, and stress.

Vesuvianite, originally found on Mount Vesuvius, is associated with fertility and goddess energy—probably because of its vibrant green color.

Wulfenite, an orange, yellow, and red stone, can fire passions and keep love burning.

Zebra stone, just as you might expect, is marked by its distinctive black and white stripes. Use it when you need to compare and contrast two or more issues, or when a situation seems to be so polarized as to be black and white.

Zircon, a beautiful, natural gemstone, is often mistaken for cubic zirconia, the laboratory-grown diamond imitation. Historically, zircon was used as a diamond substitute, and you can still use it in place of diamonds for metaphysical purposes. In addition to clear varieties, zircon is available in red, orange, yellow, green, and blue. Jacinth is a red form of zircon.

Zoisite, is typically green with a ruby-colored center. Because zoisite so often incorporates two separate stones on opposite sides of the color wheel, it can be a useful tool if you are trying to harmonize two extremes, attract new people or ideas, or work in a partnership of opposites.

Quick Reference Guides

CRYSTALS BY COLOR

Red	Alexandrite, fire opal, garnet, red carnelian, red jasper, red tiger's eye, red tourmaline, rhodochrosite, rhodonite, ruby, sard, spinel, thulite
Pink	Cobalt calcite, coral, kunzite, morganite, opal, pink agate, pink or peach aventurine, pink calcite, pink carnelian, pink danburite, pink dolomite, rose quartz, smithsonite, stilbite, thulite, unakite
Orange	Amber, orange calcite, orange carnelian, orange millennium, sunstone, tiger's eye, topaz, wulfenite
Yellow/gold	Ametrine, amber, brass, chrysoberyl, citrine, copper, golden calcite, goldstone, honey calcite, petrified wood, pyrite, sulphur, sunstone, tiger's eye, topaz, yellow jasper

Green	Actinolite, alexandrite, apophyllite, aventurine, bloodstone, chrysoprase, diopside, dioptase, emerald, epidote, green calcite, green fluorite, green obsidian, green tourmaline, hiddenite, jade, malachite, moldavite, moss agate, nephrite, peridot, prenhite, seraphinite, serpentine, unakite, variscite, vesuvianite, zoisite
Blue-green	Amazonite, aquamarine, aqua aura, azurite, blue topaz, bornite, chrysocolla, labradorite, larimar, quantum-quattro silica, turquoise
Blue	Angelite, azurite, blue chalcedony, blue goldstone, blue lace agate, blue obsidian, dumortierite, hawk's eye, kyanite, labradorite, lapis lazuli, sapphire, sodalite, tanzanite
Indigo	Apatite, charoite, hawk's eye, lapis lazuli, sugilite, tanzanite
Violet/purple	Amethyst, ametrine, charoite, iolite, lepidolite, purple fluorite, purple agate, sugilite
Black	Apache tears, black pearls, black tourmaline, Boji Stones, jet, lodestone, nebula stone, obsidian, onyx, snowflake obsidian, tektite
Brown	Andalusite, aragonite, Boji Stones, chiastolite, desert rose, flint, fulgurite, jasper, mochi marbles, smoky quartz, topaz
White	Calcite, celestite, white dolomite, howlite, moonstone, mother-of-pearl, pearl, selenite, snow quartz

Clear	Clear calcite, clear danburite, clear dolomite, clear quartz, diamond, Herkimer diamond, phenacite, ulexite, zircon
Silver	Galena, hematite, mica, muscovite, platinum, silver
Crystals that come in a variety of colors and blends	Agate, ametrine, apophyllite, beryl, bloodstone, calcite, cats' eye, fluorite, jasper, malachite, opal, peacock ore, petalite, rainbow obsidian, ruby in zoisite, sardonyx, topaz, tourmalated quartz, zebra stone

Birthstones

Month	Modern	Traditional/Ancient
January	Garnet	Garnet
February	Amethyst	Amethyst
March	Aquamarine	Bloodstone
April	Diamond	Diamond or white topaz
May	Emerald	Emerald
June	Pearl (alternates: alexandrite, moonstone)	Alexandrite, moonstone, pearl
July	Ruby	Ruby
August	Peridot, sardonyx	Peridot, sardonyx
September	Sapphire	Sapphire
October	Pink opal (alternates: rose zircon, tourmaline)	Opal, tourmaline
November	Citrine, yellow topaz	Citrine, yellow topaz
December	Turquoise	Blue topaz, blue zircon, lapis lazuli, turquoise

Planetary Correspondences

Planet	Modern	Chaldean (Mesopotamia 400 BC)
Mercury	Agate	Agate
Uranus	Aquamarine	—
Venus	Emerald, jade	Emerald
Neptune	Opal, amethyst	—
Earth	Agate	—
Pluto	Kunzite, spinel	—
Mars	Ruby, garnet, bloodstone	Ruby
Moon	Pearls, moonstone	Selenite
Jupiter	Amethyst, sapphire	Jacinth
Sun	Topaz, ruby	Diamond
Saturn	Sapphire, onyx, obsidian	Sapphire

ZODIAC STONES

Sign	Planet	Color	Corresponding crystals
Aries	Mars	Red	Alexandrite, fire opal, garnet, red carnelian, red jasper, red tiger's eye, red tourmaline, rhodochrosite, rhodonite, ruby, sard, spinel
Taurus	Venus	Green	Actinolite, alexandrite, apophyllite, aventurine, bloodstone, chrysoprase, diopside, dioptase, green calcite, emerald, epidote, green calcite, green fluorite, green obsidian, green tourmaline, jade, malachite, moldavite, moss agate, nephrite, peridot, prenhite, serpentine, unakite, variscite, vesuvianite
Gemini	Mercury	Yellow	Ametrine, amber, chrysoberyl, citrine, copper, golden calcite, goldstone, hiddenite, honey calcite, petrified wood, pyrite, sulphur, sunstone, tiger's eye, topaz, yellow jasper
Cancer	Moon	White	Calcite, celestite, white dolomite, howlite, moonstone, mother-of-pearl, pearl, selenite, snow quartz
Leo	Sun	Orange or gold	Amber, orange calcite, orange carnelian, orange millennium, sunstone, tiger's eye, topaz, wulfenite

Sign	Planet	Color	Stones
Virgo	Mercury	Blue	Angelite, azurite, blue chalcedony, blue goldstone, blue lace agate, blue obsidian, dumortierite, hawk's eye, kyanite, labradorite, lapis lazuli, sapphire
Libra	Venus	Pink	Cobalt calcite, coral, kunzite, morganite, opal, pink agate, pink or peach aventurine, pink calcite, pink carnelian, pink danburite, pink dolomite, rose quartz, smithsonite, unakite
Scorpio	Pluto	Black	Apache tears, black pearls, black tourmaline, Boji Stones, jet, lodestone, nebula stone, obsidian, onyx, snowflake obsidian, tektite
Sagittarius	Jupiter	Purple	Amethyst, ametrine, charoite, iolite, lepidolite, purple fluorite, purple agate, sugilite
Capricorn	Saturn	Brown	Andalusite, aragonite, Boji Stones, chiastolite, desert rose, flint, fulgurite, jasper, mochi marbles, smoky quartz, topaz
Aquarius	Uranus	Blue-green	Amazonite, aquamarine, aqua aura, azurite, blue topaz, chrysocolla, labradorite, larimar, peacock ore, quantum-quattro silica, turquoise
Pisces	Neptune	Indigo and purple	Indigo apatite, charoite, hawk's eye, lapis lazuli, sugilite, tanzanite; purple amethyst, ametrine, charoite, iolite, lepidolite, purple fluorite, purple agate, sugilite

Chakra Stones

Chakra	Location	Associations	Color	Crystals
1. Base or root chakra	The base of the spine	Survival issues, physical existence, and material concerns like food, clothing, and shelter	Red	Alexandrite, fire opal, garnet, red carnelian, red jasper, red tiger's eye, red tourmaline, rhodochrosite, rhodonite, ruby, sard, spinel. *Note: dark crystals like hematite, lodestone, obsidian, and onyx are often used in conjunction with the first chakra for grounding.*
2. Sacral or spleen chakra	Between the pelvic bone and the navel	Sexuality and creativity	Orange	Amber, orange calcite, orange carnelian, orange millennium, sunstone, tiger's eye, topaz, wulfenite.
3. Solar plexus chakra	Below the breastbone	Personal power	Yellow	Ametrine, amber, brass, chrysoberyl, citrine, copper, golden calcite, goldstone, hiddenite, honey calcite, petrified wood, pyrite, sulfur, sunstone, tiger's eye, topaz, yellow jasper.

Chakra	Location	Function	Color	Crystals
4. Heart chakra	The heart	Love and emotion	Green	Actinolite, alexandrite, apophyllite, aventurine, bloodstone, chrysoprase, diopside, dioptase, green calcite, emerald, epidote, green calcite, green fluorite, green obsidian, green tourmaline, jade, malachite, moldavite, moss agate, nephrite, peridot, prehnite, serpentine, unakite, variscite, vesuvianite.
5. Throat chakra	The throat	Communication	Blue	Angelite, azurite, blue chalcedony, blue goldstone, blue lace agate, blue obsidian, dumortierite, hawk's eye, kyanite, labradorite, lapis lazuli, sapphire.
6. Third eye chakra	Forehead	Imagination and psychic ability	Indigo	Apatite, charoite, hawk's eye, lapis lazuli, sugilite, tanzanite.
7. Crown chakra	Just above the head	Spirituality	Violet	Amethyst, ametrine, charoite, iolite, lepidolite, purple fluorite, purple agate, sugilite. *Note: because of its association with the spirit, you can also use clear crystals on the seventh chakra, such as clear quartz, danburite, Herkimer diamonds, and selenite.*

To Attract or Enhance

Abundance	Abundance crystals
Anything	Lodestone, magnetite
Calm	Rose quartz
Communication	Blue and blue-green stones for the throat chakra: amazonite, aqua aura, aquamarine, blue lace agate, turquoise
Confidence and courage	Agate, bloodstone, calcite, carnelian, charoite, diamond, hematite, tiger's eye
Creativity	Yellow for intellect: calcite, citrine, opal, topaz; green for fertility and growth: amazonite
Energy	Fiery red and orange stones: carnelian, garnet, red jasper
Family harmony	Clusters
Friendship	Chrysoprase, rose quartz, pink tourmaline, turquoise
General health	Green stones like emerald, aventurine, green calcite, green tourmaline, malachite
Happiness	Sunny, optimistic stones like orange calcite, chrysoprase, sunstone, unakite; soothing blue kyanite and peacock ore; rose quartz
Healthy plants	Green stones like green agate, moss agate, jade, malachite
Intellect	Structured geometric stones like fluorite, pyrite

Love	Romantic stones: alexandrite, amber, amethyst, chrysocolla, diamond, emerald, jade, lapis lazuli, lapidolite, malachite, moonstone, opal, pearl, rose quartz, rhodochrosite, rhodonite, sapphire, topaz, pink tourmaline, watermelon tourmaline, turquoise
Marriage and relationships	Any twin crystal, and any blended stone with two contrasting colors: ametrine, dalmatian jasper, malachite, mochi marbles, ruby in zoisite, rutilated quartz, sodalite, snowflake obsidian, tourmalated quartz, unakite, watermelon tourmaline
Money	Green stones like aventurine, chrysoprase, emerald, green tourmaline, jade, malachite, or golden stones like citrine, golden calcite, pyrite, and tiger's eye
Patience	Soothing, calming pinks: rhodonite
Pleasant dreams	The colors of twilight: amethyst, azurite, citrine, moonstone, opal, selenite
Pregnancy	Geodes, which seem to be pregnant with microcrystalline formations; stones with goddess associations, such as moonstone and selenite; unakite
Psychic ability	Amethyst, clear quartz
Safe travel by sea	Aquamarine, coral, larimar, pearl
Safe travel by air	grounding stones like black tourmaline, hematite, obsidian, and smoky quartz; celestial stones like celestite, blue lace agate; visionary stones like hawk's eye
Sex	Passionate red crystals like ruby, garnet, and shiva lingam stones

To Repel or Eliminate

Addiction   Amethyst

Anger   Amethyst, carnelian, chrysocolla, emerald, green
              calcite, green tourmaline, lepidolite, topaz

Anxiety   Rose quartz, rhodochrosite, rhodonite, peridot,
              aventurine

Depression   Blue agate, kunzite, amber, topaz

Fear   Charoite, smoky quartz

Grief   Apache tears

Heartbreak   Rose quartz

Jealousy   Peridot, chrysoprase

Nightmares   Amethyst, holed stones

Stress   Grounding stones like black tourmaline,
              hematite, obsidian, smoky quartz; calming
              stones like rhodochrosite, rhodonite

Glossary

Active meditation. A dynamic and lively form of meditation that usually involves physical movement.

Acupressure. A hands-on form of alternative healing.

Acupuncture. A method of treating illness by inserting needles into the body's meridians.

Adamantine. Smooth, reflective, and polished.

Adularescence. A milky, flashy sheen created by microscopic inclusions.

Affirmations. A form of practical magic that works on both a conscious and subconscious level by retraining the brain to think in positive terms.

Aggregates. A combination of microscopic crystals.

Akashic Record. The cosmic repository of all knowledge.

Alloy. A mixture of two or more metals, or a mixture of a metal and another substance.

Amorphous. A substance without a clearly defined structure.

Amulets. Tokens and charms that can be worn for protection; they are intended to keep bad things away.

Ancient elements. Earth, water, air, and fire.

Anthraxolite. Petrified plant life, which may resemble specks of black coal.

Assembled. Produced from two or more separate crystals.

Asterism. A star-shaped reflection that appears when some gemstones are cut.

Astral plane. A spiritual level of reality, filled with thoughts and mental imagery.

Astral travel. A meditative exercise in which the consciousness actually leaves the body and travels through space and time in the astral plane.

Aura. The natural electromagnetic field that surrounds the human body.

Aventurescence. A reflective sheen caused by small metallic inclusions. Aventurine, sunstone, and goldstone are aventurescent.

Axis. The straight line through a crystal that defines its symmetry.

Bleached. Chemically lightened or removed.

Bonded. Fused with a colorless bonding agent.

Cabochon. A stone with a flat bottom and a domed surface.

Cairns. Pyramid-shaped piles of stones to serve as a focal point for energy.

Carat. A unit of measure used to weight gemstones; a carat is one-fifth of a gram.

Chakra. Sanskrit for "wheel" or "disk." The chakras make up the energy system of the human body.

Channeling. The act of connecting and communicating with the spiritual realm.

Chatoyancy. The cat's eye effect in some crystals, in which a shimmering band of light moves across the surface of a stone.

Clarity. The relative clearness of a crystal and the absence of inclusions.

Clearing. The process of erasing programs or impressions from a crystal.

Cleavage. The natural plane of weakness in a mineral where it will split.

Coated. Lacquered, enameled, inked, foiled, or otherwise treated for better color, improved appearance, or special effects.

Collective unconscious. The bond of shared emotion and understanding that unites all people on a psychic level and the well of shared myth, history, and legendary associations.

Crystal. A solid in which the atoms or molecules are arranged in a definite, repeating pattern.

Crystalline. Any substances with a precise atomic arrangement.

Crystalomancy. The art of reading a crystal ball.

Devas. Nature spirits.

Diffraction. The process of splitting white light into a spectrum of colors.

Diffused. Treated with chemicals and high temperatures, to change their color or to produce special effects.

Dispersion. The process of splitting white light into a spectrum of colors.

Dodecahedron. A solid with twelve sides, each one a perfect, five-sided pentagram.

Dowsing. Divination with a pendulum.

Dyed. Recolored or color treated.

Elementals. The devic embodiment of the four ancient elements. Earth elementals are gnomes, and their numbers can include elves and brownies. Air elements are sylphs, including fairies and cherubs. Fire elementals are salamanders, flaming creatures that usually look like lizards or balls of light. Water elementals are undines, such as nymphs, mermaids, and water spirits.

Elixir. A magical healing substance.

Enhydro. Literally, "water within." Enhydro crystals contain pockets of liquid trapped inside the crystal during its formation.

Face. Any facet or flat surface on a crystal.

Facet. Any face or flat surface on a crystal.

Filled or infilled. Augmented with glass, plastic, or other stabilizing material.

Gamma or electron irradiated. Subjected to gamma and/or electron bombardment.

Geode. A rock with a crystal-lined cavity.

Granular. Grainy.

Greasy. An oily luster.

Grid. A framework for laying crystals and stones during a healing session.

Hardness. Scratch-resistance.

Heat-treated. Heated to change their color, clarity, or phenomena. Sapphire, ruby, tanzanite, citrine, and aquamarine are commonly enhanced by heat treatment.

Hexagonal crystals. Six-sided prisms or pyramids.

Hexahedron. A cube with six sides, each one a perfect square.

Hue. Color. The human eye can distinguish 150 different hues, including all the colors of the rainbow—red, orange, yellow, green, blue, indigo, and violet.

Icosahedron. A solid with twenty sides, each one a perfect, equilateral triangle.

Idiochromatic. Color that is inherent due to chemical composition and structure.

Igneous rocks. Formed from erupted volcanic lava or solidified magma.

Inclusions. Trapped particles of foreign matter, such as dirt, dust, other minerals, or pockets of water or oil.

Iridescence. A rainbow-like color effect.

Isometric crystal. A cube-shaped crystal with four equal sides.

Lasered. Treated with lasers.

Lucid dreaming. Conscious dreaming.

Luster. The overall shine of a gemstone, determined by the way it reflects light.

Mandala. A colorful, circular design that represents the shape and the creation of the universe.

Matrix. The base or foundation rock on which a crystal grows.

Meridians. The intersecting lines and pathways that connect the chakras.

Metamorphic rock. Any rock formed by the action of heat, pressure, or permeation by other substances on preexisting rock material.

Microcrystalline. A mineral structure in which crystals are too small to be detected by the naked eye.

Mohs Scale. A method of classifying the relative hardness of minerals.

Monoclinic crystal. A crystal shaped like a short, stubby parallelogram with tilted faces at each end.

Obelisks. Four-sided pillars that terminate in a pyramid shape.

Octahedron. A solid with eight sides, each one a perfect, equilateral triangle.

Oiled and resin-infused. Treated with colorless oil, wax, natural resin, or other material.

Opalescence. A milky-blue shimmer.

Opaque. Not transparent or translucent.

Organic gems. Crystalline materials made by or derived from living organisms, such as amber.

Orthorhombic crystal. A crystal shaped like a short, wide rectangle, or rhomboid.

Pendulum. Any object on a string used for dowsing and divination.

Piezoelectric crystal. A mineral that vibrates regularly when an electric current passes through it.

Piezoelectricity. The electric current some crystals produce when they are squeezed.

Pleochroic gems. Stones that display one color from one direction but exhibit one or more other colors or shades when seen from another direction.

Polycrystalline. Consisting of many small crystals.

Program. To instill a plan or design into a crystal.

Pyroelectricity. The electric current some crystals produce as a result of temperature changes.

Reflective meditation. A calming, quiet, and passive form of meditation. For Westerners, it comes closest to Zen meditation, in which the goal is to forget oneself and experience the universe as a whole.

Refraction. The bending of light.

Resonance. A vibration that occurs in response to other frequencies in the area.

Rhombohedron. A six-sided prism.

Rock. A conglomerate of many minerals, chemicals, and solid organic materials that come from inside the earth.

Rough. An uncut, unpolished crystal.

Runes. An ancient magical alphabet of Northern Europe.

Rutile. A mineral that forms needle-like inclusions inside other types of minerals and crystals.

Sacred geometry. The study of mathematics as a path to God.

Saturation. Purity of color. Crystals that have a lot of gray or brown are less saturated with other colors, and they look dull as a result. Likewise, crystals that are too light are poorly saturated, too, because they look washed out.

Scintillation. Sparkle.

Scrying. Divination with a crystal ball or any smooth, reflective surface.

Sedimentary rock. The hardened sediment of other rock fragments, organic materials, and other substances.

Semitranslucent. Transmits a limited amount of light.

Semitransparent. Transmits most light through a substance.

Specific gravity. The density of a crystal, calculated by comparing its weight with the weight of an equal volume of water.

Star effect. A reflection that looks like intersecting bands of light across the surface of a gem. Rubies, sapphires, and garnets often display a star effect.

Stones. Short for gemstones.

Gemstones. Crystals that can be cut and polished for jewelry.

Streak. The color a powered mineral on an unglazed white tile; a method of identifying minerals.

Striation. A parallel scratch, groove, or line.

Submetallic. Opaque and generally nonreflective.

Symmetry. Balanced proportion.

Synchronicity. Meaningful coincidence.

Synthetic. Man-made.

Tabular. Flat, like a table.

Talismans. Good luck charms.

Termination. The point at the tip of a crystal.

Tetragonal crystal. A crystal shaped like a long, tall rectangle.

Tetrahedron. A triangular pyramid with four sides, each one a perfect, equilateral triangle.

Tone. The relative lightness or darkness of a hue.

Totems. Objects carved in the shape of animals or mythical creatures.

Translucent. Allows light to pass through.

Transparency. How well light passes through a crystal.

Transparent. Clear as window glass.

Trapeziums. A crystal that looks like a pyramid with its top cut off.

Treatment. Any technique used to enhance a crystal or gemstone, such as heating, bleaching, dying, diffusing, and irradiating.

Triclinic. Flat with sharp edges, but no right angles.

Trigonal crystal. A crystal with three equilateral sides.

Vitrious. Glassy.

Vugs. Small cavities formed inside rock when crystals erode and leave a void behind.

Waxed and oiled. Impregnated with colorless wax, paraffin, and oil.

Bibliography

Books

Andrews, Ted. *Crystal Balls & Crystal Bowls*. St. Paul, MN: Llewellyn Publications, 1995.

Arcarti, Kristyna. *Gems and Crystals for Beginners*. London: Hodder & Stoughton, 1994.

Cunningham, Scott. *Cunningham's Encyclopedia of Crystal, Gem & Metal Magic*. St. Paul, MN: Llewellyn Publications, 1998 and 2002.

Darling, Peter. *Crystals*. London: Quintet Publishing, 1998.

Dow, JaneAnn. *Crystal Journey: Travel Guide for the New Shaman*. Santa Fe, NM: Journey Books, 1994.

Eden, Donna. *The Energy Medicine Kit*. Boulder, CO: Sounds True, Inc., 2004.

Elsbeth, Marguerite. *Crystal Medicine*. St. Paul, MN: Llewellyn Publications, 1997.

Galde, Phyllis. *Crystal Healing: The Next Step*. St. Paul, MN: Llewellyn Publications, 1988.

Gribbin, John. *Quantum Physics: A Beginner's Guide to the Sub-atomic World*. New York: Dorling Kindersley Limited, 2002.

Hall, Judy. *The Crystal Bible: A Definitive Guide to Crystals.*
Cincinnati: Walking Stick Press, 2004.

Harold, Edmund. *Focus on Crystals.* New York: Ballantine
Books, 1986.

Harrison, Stephanie and Barbara Kleiner. *The Crystal Wisdom
Kit.* Boston: Journey Editions, 1997.

Jangl, Alda Marian and James Francis Jangl. *Ancient Legends of
Gems and Jewels.* Coeur d'Alene, ID: Prisma Press, 1985.

Judith, Anodea. *The Truth About Chakras.* St. Paul, MN:
Llewellyn Publications, 1994.

Kunz, George Frederick. *The Curious Lore of Precious Stones.*
New York: Dover Publications, 1971.

Melody. *Love Is in the Earth.* Wheat Ridge, CO: Earth-Love
Publishing House, 1995.

Morwyn. *The Complete Book of Psychic Arts.* St. Paul, MN:
Llewellyn Publications, 1999.

Ozaniec, Naomi. *Basic Meditation.* New York: Dorling Kindersley Limited, 1997.

Pellant, Chris. *Rocks and Minerals.* New York: Dorling Kindersley Limited, 1992.

Raphaell, Katrina. *Crystal Enlightenment: The Transforming
Properties of Crystals and Healing Stones..* Santa Fe, NM:
Aurora Press, 1985.

Spangler, David. *Blessing: The Art and the Practice.* New York:
Riverhead Books, 2001.

Sullivan, Kevin. *The Crystal Handbook.* New York: Signet, 1987.

Toy, Fiona. *Auras and Chakras: Harnessing the Energy Within.*
New York: Landsdowne Publishing, 2002.

Walker, Barbara. *The Book of Sacred Stones*. San Francisco: Harper, 1989.

Young, Evelyn M. *Dreams*. Boston: Element Books, 1998.

Zim, Herbert S. and Paul R. Shaffer. *Rocks and Minerals*. New York: Golden Press, 1957.

Websites

http://crystalsandjewelry.com. Robyn Harton, a jewelry designer and master teacher of Reiki, has posted a plethora of crystal and gem information on her site, including the metaphysical properties of many crystals, chakra information, and healing grid layouts.

http://mineral.galleries.com. The Mineral Gallery, a scientific database, provides multiple cross-linked indexes of common minerals listed by class and by group, along with detailed descriptions, characteristics, and photos.

http://mineralminers.com. Visit Mineral Miners online, and you'll be visiting a virtual gallery with thousands of images of unique mineral specimens, crystals, gemstones, lapidary rough, mineral spheres, jewelry, and other handcrafted gem and mineral gift ideas from mines and lapidary shops around the world.

http://rainbowcrystal.com. Beyond the Rainbow, a site run by Connie Barrett and Joyce Kaessinger, features a wide range of articles about crystals, including detailed information about dozens of popular crystals and specific recommendations for their use. Their first-person experiences and insights are especially useful.

http://rings-things.com. Rings and Things is a bead retailer that offers detailed descriptions of hundreds of gemstones, along with definitions, history, and photos.

http://www.thaigem.com. While the site is aimed at gemstone buyers, thaigem offers a wide range of information for metaphysical crystal shoppers, too.

Index

FREE CATALOGUE

Read unique articles by Llewellyn authors, recommendations by experts, and information on new releases. To receive a **free** copy of Llewellyn's consumer magazine, *New Worlds of Mind & Spirit,* simply call 1-877-NEW-WRLD or visit our website at www.llewellyn.com and click on *New Worlds.*

☽ LLEWELLYN ORDERING INFORMATION

 Order Online:
Visit our website at www.llewellyn.com, select your books, and order them on our secure server.

 Order by Phone:
- Call toll-free within the U.S. at 1-877-NEW-WRLD (1-877-639-9753). Call toll-free within Canada at 1-866-NEW-WRLD (1-866-639-9753)
- We accept VISA, MasterCard, and American Express

 Order by Mail:
Send the full price of your order (MN residents add 7% sales tax) in U.S. funds, plus postage & handling to:
Llewellyn Worldwide
2143 Wooddale Drive, Dept. 0-7387-0755-4
Woodbury, MN 55125-2989, U.S.A.

Postage & Handling:

Standard (U.S., Mexico, & Canada). If your order is:
$24.99 and under, add $3.00
$25.00 and over, FREE STANDARD SHIPPING

AK, HI, PR: $15.00 for one book plus $1.00 for each additional book.

International Orders (airmail only):
$16.00 for one book plus $3.00 for each additional book

Orders are processed within 2 business days.
Please allow for normal shipping time. Postage and handling rates subject to change.

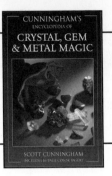

Cunningham's Encyclopedia of Crystal, Gem & Metal Magic

SCOTT CUNNINGHAM

Here you will find the most complete information anywhere on the magical qualities of more than one hundred crystals and gemstones as well as several metals. The information for each crystal, gem, or metal includes its related energy, planetary rulership, magical element, deities, tarot card, and the magical powers that each is believed to possess. Also included is a complete description of their uses for magical purposes. The classic on the subject.

0-87542-126-1
240 pp., 6 x 9, illus. $14.95

Spanish edition:
Enciclopedia de cristales, gemas y metales mágicos
1-56718-189-9 $12.95

To order, call 1-877-NEW-WRLD
Prices subject to change without notice

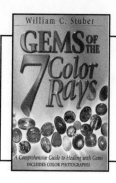

Gems of the Seven Color Rays
A Comprehensive Guide to Healing with Gems

WILLIAM STUBER

Gemstones are powerful, compact carriers of vibrational energy. This guide presents simple, step-by-step instructions for creating profound and lasting changes by working with gemstones. Learn how to use the healing properties of fifty-eight gemstones to reduce stress, release past traumas and energy blockages, and ease emotional reactions. Discover your primary color ray and how to create inner harmony and balance with these ancient gifts from the earth..

1-56718-685-8

480 pp., color insert, biblio., index $24.95

To order, call 1-877-NEW-WRLD
Prices subject to change without notice

Sacred Signs

Hear, See & Believe Messages from the Universe

ADRIAN CALABRESE, PH.D.

When popular author Adrian Calabrese's father was in surgery for a life-threatening medical condition, she asked for a sign that he would survive—and she immediately received one. Now she shares her secrets for getting clear guidance from the Universe in *Sacred Signs*, teaching readers a simple three-step method for receiving divine messages.

Unlike other books on the subject, *Sacred Signs* is not a "sign dictionary." Calabrese believes that the interpretation of a sign is as unique as the individual receiving it. The original checklists and questionnaires throughout the book help readers focus their desires to more effectively communicate with the Universe. Success stories throughout the book provide inspiration and further demonstrate how to use this personal, nondenominational approach to interpreting divine signs.

0-7387-0776-7
216 pp., 7½ x 9⅛ $12.95

To order, call 1-877-NEW-WRLD
Prices subject to change without notice

Feng Shui in Five Minutes
SELENA SUMMERS

To prosper, is it better to live in a small house in a wealthy area or a large house in a less expensive area? How can a radio, television set, or computer be a feng shui cure? What are the luckiest shapes for blocks of land?

These are just three of the many questions you'll find answered in *Feng Shui in Five Minutes*. Learn intriguing no-cost methods to improve your luck, a mystic way to hurry house sales, ancient techniques to win more dates, the Nine Celestial Cures, common feng shui faults, and much more.

0-7387-0291-9
240 pp., 5³⁄₁₆ x 8   **$12.95**

Spanish edition:
Feng Shui práctico y al instante
0-7387-0292-7   **$12.95**

How to Heal with Color
TED ANDREWS

Now, for perhaps the first time, color therapy is placed within the grasp of the average individual. Anyone can learn to facilitate and accelerate the healing process on all levels with the simple color therapies in *How to Heal with Color*.

This book provides color application guidelines that are beneficial for over fifty physical conditions and a wide variety of emotional and mental conditions. Receive simple and tangible instructions for performing "muscle testing" on yourself and others to find the most beneficial colors. Learn how to apply color therapy through touch, projection, breathing, cloth, water, and candles. Learn how to use the little known but powerful color-healing system of the mystical Qabala to balance and open the psychic centers. Plus, discover simple techniques for performing long distance healings on others.

0-7387-0811-9
176 pp., 5³⁄₁₆ x 7⅝, illus.   **$7.95**

DISCOVER WORLD UPON WORLD OF MAGIC AND WONDER

with Llewellyn's For Beginners series

Topics in the For Beginners series include:

Bach Flower Remedies	*Reiki*
Ancient Teachings	*Tarot*
Aura Reading	*Dowsing*
Divination	*Hypnosis*
Chi Kung	*Numerology*
Chakras	*Palm Reading*
I Ching	*Psychic Development*

For a complete list of over two dozen titles in this series,
please visit www.llewellyn.com

To Write to the Author

If you wish to contact the author or would like more information about this book, please write to the author in care of Llewellyn Worldwide and we will forward your request. Both the author and publisher appreciate hearing from you and learning of your enjoyment of this book and how it has helped you. Llewellyn Worldwide cannot guarantee that every letter written to the author can be answered, but all will be forwarded. Please write to:

Corrine Kenner
% Llewellyn Worldwide
2143 Wooddale Drive, Dept. 0-7387-0755-4
Woodbury, MN 55125-2989, U.S.A.

Please enclose a self-addressed stamped envelope for reply,
or $1.00 to cover costs. If outside U.S.A., enclose
international postal reply coupon.

Many of Llewellyn's authors have websites with additional information and resources. For more information, please visit our website at:

www.llewellyn.com